Dante's
Inferno
In Plain and Simple English

BookCaps™ Study Guide
www.bookcaps.com

© 2011. All Rights Reserved.

Cover image © dundanim - Fotolia.com

Table of Contents

About This Series 3

Inferno: Canto I 4

Inferno: Canto II 8

Inferno: Canto III 12

Inferno: Canto IV 16

Inferno: Canto V 21

Inferno: Canto VI..25

Inferno: Canto VII...29

Inferno: Canto VIII 33

Inferno: Canto IX..37

Inferno: Canto X 41

Inferno: Canto XI..45

Inferno: Canto XII 49

Inferno: Canto XIII 53

Inferno: Canto XIV...58

Inferno: Canto XV 62

Inferno: Canto XVI...66

Inferno: Canto XVII..70

Inferno: Canto XVIII...74

Inferno: Canto XIX...78

Inferno: Canto XX 82

Inferno: Canto XXI...86

Inferno: Canto XXII 90

Inferno: Canto XXIII...95

Inferno: Canto XXIV...100

Inferno: Canto XXV 105

Inferno: Canto XXVI...110

Inferno: Canto XXVII 114

Inferno: Canto XXVIII...118

Inferno: Canto XXIX...122

Inferno: Canto XXX 126

Inferno: Canto XXXI...131

Inferno: Canto XXXII 136

Inferno: Canto XXXIII...140

Inferno: Canto XXXIV **145**

About This Series

The "Classic Retold" series started as a way of telling classics for the modern reader—being careful to preserve the themes and integrity of the original. Whether you want to understand Shakespeare a little more or are trying to get a better grasps of the Greek classics, there is a book waiting for you!

The series is expanding every month. Visit BookCaps.com to see all the books in the series, and while you are there join the Facebook page, so you are first to know when a new book comes out.

INFERNO

Inferno: Canto I

Midway upon the journey of our life
I found myself within a forest dark,
For the straightforward pathway had been lost.

Ah me! how hard a thing it is to say
What was this forest savage, rough, and stern,

Which in the very thought renews the fear.

So bitter is it, death is little more;
But of the good to treat, which there I found,
Speak will I of the other things I saw there.
I cannot well repeat how there I entered,
So full was I of slumber at the moment
In which I had abandoned the true way.

But after I had reached a mountain's foot,
At that point where the valley terminated,
Which had with consternation pierced my heart,

Upward I looked, and I beheld its shoulders,
Vested already with that planet's rays
Which leadeth others right by every road.

Then was the fear a little quieted
That in my heart's lake had endured throughout
The night, which I had passed so piteously.

And even as he, who, with distressful breath,
Forth issued from the sea upon the shore,
Turns to the water perilous and gazes;

So did my soul, that still was fleeing onward,
Turn itself back to re-behold the pass
Which never yet a living person left.

After my weary body I had rested,
The way resumed I on the desert slope,
So that the firm foot ever was the lower.
And lo! almost where the ascent began,
A panther light and swift exceedingly,

Half-way through the journey of my life
I found myself in a dark forest,
Having lost the main path.

"Oh me!" I said,
Upon seeing the savage, rough, and unforgiving forest.
My sense of fear was renewed.

Death is bitter,
But can be good, which is what I found.
I will also tell of the other things I saw there.
I can't say how I entered.
I was so tired,
When I strayed from the main road.

But after I reached the foot of the mountain,
Where the valley ends.
My heart was pierced with anxiety.

I looked up at its enormity.
It seemed to rise up to the moon,
Which leads others faithfully on every road.

The fear inside me subsided,
That had endured throughout
The night which passed so wretchedly.

Like the one whose breath
Brought forth the sea and shore,
Turns back to see his creation.

My soul fleeing forward
Turned back to behold the place
Where a living person could not leave.

After I had rested my weary body,
I resumed my way upwards,
Climbing steadily with one foot below the other.
Behold! Where I began to climb,
I saw a silent panther light and swift,

Which with a spotted skin was covered o'er!
And never moved she from before my face,
Nay, rather did impede so much my way,
That many times I to return had turned.

The time was the beginning of the morning,
And up the sun was mounting with those stars
That with him were, what time the Love Divine

At first in motion set those beauteous things;

So were to me occasion of good hope,
The variegated skin of that wild beast,

The hour of time, and the delicious season;
But not so much, that did not give me fear
A lion's aspect which appeared to me.

He seemed as if against me he were coming
With head uplifted, and with ravenous hunger,
So that it seemed the air was afraid of him;

And a she-wolf, that with all hungerings
Seemed to be laden in her meagreness,
And many folk has caused to live forlorn!

She brought upon me so much heaviness,
With the affright that from her aspect came,
That I the hope relinquished of the height.

And as he is who willingly acquires,
And the time comes that causes him to lose,
Who weeps in all his thoughts and is despondent,

E'en such made me that beast withouten peace,
Which, coming on against me by degrees
Thrust me back thither where the sun is silent.

While I was rushing downward to the lowland,
Before mine eyes did one present himself,
Who seemed from long-continued silence hoarse.

When I beheld him in the desert vast,
"Have pity on me," unto him I cried,
"Whiche'er thou art, or shade or real man!"

He answered me: "Not man; man once I was,

With spotted skin.
She never moved from in front of me.
Instead she seemed to guide me,
As I turned.

It was early in the morning
When the sun resides with the stars.
In such a lovely and divine time

That the first motion that began these beautiful things
Gave me hope.
So did the variegated skin of that wild beast,

The time of day and the delicious season,
But not so much that I was without fear.
Then a figure like a lion appeared to me

He seemed as if he were coming for me.
His head held high and hungry looking,
So even the air felt afraid.

Then I saw a she-wolf
Whose hunger caused by man
Overwhelmed her small body.

The sight of her made me so sad
When I saw her,
I gave up all hope.

And like a man who willingly gets,
And the time that comes causing him to lose
I wept.

I was without peace,
Which came on me little by little,
Causing me to look back.

While I ran down,
I saw a man
Who seemed unable to talk.

When I saw him in the open,
I cried, "Have pity on me,
If you are real or just a vision."

He answered, "I was once a man, although I am no more.

And both my parents were of Lombardy,
And Mantuans by country both of them.

My parents were from Lombardy.
They were both Mantuans.

'Sub Julio' was I born, though it was late,
And lived at Rome under the good Augustus,
During the time of false and lying gods.

I was born in Rome during the latter part of Julius
And lived under the leader Augustus,
During the time of false and lying gods.

A poet was I, and I sang that just
Son of Anchises, who came forth from Troy,
After that Ilion the superb was burned.

I was a poet and I sang about
Son of Anchises, who came from Troy,
After the city of Ilion burned.

But thou, why goest thou back to such annoyance?
Why climb'st thou not the Mount Delectable,
Which is the source and cause of every joy?"

But why are you going back to such annoyance?
Why aren't you climbing Mount Delectable,
The source and cause of every joy?"

"Now, art thou that Virgilius and that fountain
Which spreads abroad so wide a river of speech?"
I made response to him with bashful forehead.

"Aren't you the famous Virgil,
The writer who is known so well for his speech?"
I responded shyly.

"O, of the other poets honour and light,
Avail me the long study and great love
That have impelled me to explore thy volume!

"Oh, I honor the other poets,
Who inspired my long study and great love
Of your work!

Thou art my master, and my author thou,
Thou art alone the one from whom I took
The beautiful style that has done honour to me.

You are my master and I am your author.
Your art alone is the father of my style
That has done me so well.

Behold the beast, for which I have turned back;
Do thou protect me from her, famous Sage,
For she doth make my veins and pulses tremble."

Look at the beast for which I have retreated.
Protect me from her, famous Sage
For she makes me tremble with fear."

"Thee it behoves to take another road,"
Responded he, when he beheld me weeping,
"If from this savage place thou wouldst escape;

"Then it would be wise to take another road,"
He responded, when he saw me weeping.
"If you want to escape this savage place

Because this beast, at which thou criest out,
Suffers not any one to pass her way,
But so doth harass him, that she destroys him;

Because of this beast you are crying over
Does not kill anyone who passes her way,
But worries them to death.

And has a nature so malign and ruthless,
That never doth she glut her greedy will,
And after food is hungrier than before.

She is so ruthless
That she is never satisfied,
And after she eats, she is hungrier than before.

Many the animals with whom she weds,
And more they shall be still, until the Greyhound
Comes, who shall make her perish in her pain.

Many animals that pass her way,
And there will be more, until the Greyhound
Comes who will kill her.

He shall not feed on either earth or pelf,

He will not feed on her,

But upon wisdom, and on love and virtue;
'Twixt Feltro and Feltro shall his nation be;

Of that low Italy shall he be the saviour,
On whose account the maid Camilla died,
Euryalus, Turnus, Nisus, of their wounds;

Through every city shall he hunt her down,
Until he shall have driven her back to Hell,
There from whence envy first did let her loose.

Therefore I think and judge it for thy best
Thou follow me, and I will be thy guide,
And lead thee hence through the eternal place,

Where thou shalt hear the desperate lamentations,
Shalt see the ancient spirits disconsolate,
Who cry out each one for the second death;

And thou shalt see those who contented are
Within the fire, because they hope to come,
Whene'er it may be, to the blessed people;

To whom, then, if thou wishest to ascend,
A soul shall be for that than I more worthy;
With her at my departure I will leave thee;

Because that Emperor, who reigns above,
In that I was rebellious to his law,
Wills that through me none come into his city.

He governs everywhere, and there he reigns;
There is his city and his lofty throne;
O happy he whom thereto he elects!"

And I to him: "Poet, I thee entreat,
By that same God whom thou didst never know,
So that I may escape this woe and worse,

Thou wouldst conduct me there where thou hast said,
That I may see the portal of Saint Peter,
And those thou makest so disconsolate."

Then he moved on, and I behind him followed.

But upon wisdom, love and virtue,
He will build his nation between the Feltros.

He will be the savior of Italy,
The reason maid Camilla,
Euryalus, Turnus, and Nisus died.

He will hunt her down,
Until he drives her back to Hell,
Where she was released by envy.

Therefore, I think it will be best,
If you follow me and let me be your guide
To lead you through the eternal place,

Where you will hear the desperate cries
And see ancient miserable spirits,
Who cry out for a second death.

You will also see those who are contented
Within the fire because they hope to come
To the blessed people at some time.

Then, if you wish to come up,
A soul more worthy will accompany you.
At that time, I will leave you.

Because the Emperor, who reigns above,
And because I was rebellious to his law
Won't let anyone come to his city through me.

He rules everywhere and he reigns
In his city upon a lofty throne.
Oh, the ones he allows there are so happy."

I said to him, "Poet, I beg you,
In the name of the God you never knew,
So I may escape this horror and more

You would take me there,
So I may see the gate of Saint Peter
And avoid the unhappy ones."

Then he moved on, and I followed him.

Inferno: Canto II

Day was departing, and the embrowned air
Released the animals that are on earth
From their fatigues; and I the only one

As the day was ending and the time
When nocturnal animals
Awake from their slumber, and I being the only one

Made myself ready to sustain the war,
Both of the way and likewise of the woe,
Which memory that errs not shall retrace.

Made myself ready for war
In the way and the sorrow,
Which my memory will retain.

O Muses, O high genius, now assist me!
O memory, that didst write down what I saw,
Here thy nobility shall be manifest!

Oh Muses, Oh great geniuses, assist me now!
Oh memory, that wrote down what I saw,
Your nobility will be recorded here.

And I began: "Poet, who guidest me,
Regard my manhood, if it be sufficient,
Ere to the arduous pass thou dost confide me.

So I began: "Poet, who guided me,
Think of my manhood and if it is sufficient,
Tell me the way.

Thou sayest, that of Silvius the parent,
While yet corruptible, unto the world
Immortal went, and was there bodily.

You say Silvio's parent,
Although corruptible in the world,
Went to the immortal realm and remained in body.

But if the adversary of all evil
Was courteous, thinking of the high effect
That issue would from him, and who, and what,

But if the adversary of all evil
Was kind, thinking the effect,
That would come from him,

To men of intellect unmeet it seems not;
For he was of great Rome, and of her empire
In the empyreal heaven as father chosen;

Offered to all men, it seems impossible,
For he was for Rome and her empire,
Chosen by the heavenly father;

The which and what, wishing to speak the truth,
Were stablished as the holy place, wherein
Sits the successor of the greatest Peter.

The whole truth,
Established in the holy place,
Sits, the successor of the greatest Peter.

Upon this journey, whence thou givest him vaunt,
Things did he hear, which the occasion were
Both of his victory and the papal mantle.

Upon this journey, when you boasted about him,
He heard things
About his victory and the papal mantle.

Thither went afterwards the Chosen Vessel,
To bring back comfort thence unto that Faith,
Which of salvation's way is the beginning.

Afterwards the Chosen Vessel went,
To bring comfort to anyone of the faith,
Which marks the beginning of salvation.

But I, why thither come, or who concedes it?
I not Aeneas am, I am not Paul,

As for me, why am I coming or who allows it?
I am not Aeneas or Paul,

Nor I, nor others, think me worthy of it.

Therefore, if I resign myself to come,
I fear the coming may be ill-advised;
Thou'rt wise, and knowest better than I speak."

And as he is, who unwills what he willed,
And by new thoughts doth his intention change,
So that from his design he quite withdraws,

Such I became, upon that dark hillside,

Because, in thinking, I consumed the emprise,
Which was so very prompt in the beginning.

"If I have well thy language understood,"
Replied that shade of the Magnanimous,
"Thy soul attainted is with cowardice,

Which many times a man encumbers so,
It turns him back from honoured enterprise,
As false sight doth a beast, when he is shy.

That thou mayst free thee from this apprehension,
I'll tell thee why I came, and what I heard
At the first moment when I grieved for thee.

Among those was I who are in suspense,
And a fair, saintly Lady called to me
In such wise, I besought her to command me.

Her eyes where shining brighter than the Star;
And she began to say, gentle and low,
With voice angelical, in her own language:

'O spirit courteous of Mantua,
Of whom the fame still in the world endures,
And shall endure, long-lasting as the world;

A friend of mine, and not the friend of fortune,
Upon the desert slope is so impeded
Upon his way, that he has turned through terror,
And may, I fear, already be so lost,
That I too late have risen to his succour,
From that which I have heard of him in Heaven.

Bestir thee now, and with thy speech ornate,
And with what needful is for his release,

I do not think I am worthy.

Therefore, if I agree to come,
I fear it may be for the wrong reasons;
You are wise and know more than I am able to
say."
And like one who changes his mind,
And rethinks his intentions,
So that he stops his journey,

Upon that dark hillside, I was rethinking this
journey,
Because when I thought about it,
I was ready in the beginning.

"If I understand you,"
Replied the magnanimous poet,
"You are a cowardly soul,

Which often compels a man many times,
So, it turns him back from honorable activities,
Like a shy beast.

So, you are not inhibited from this journey,
I'll tell you why I came and what I heard
At the first moment I felt sorry for you.

I was among the souls held in Purgatory,
And a fair, saintly Lady called to me
In such a wise way, I told her I was hers to
command.
Her eyes were brighter than the Star;
And she began to say with a gentle, low
And angelic voice, in her own language:

'Oh spirit of Mantua,
Whose fame still endures in the world,
And shall outlast the world;

A friend of mine, and not a friend of fortune,
Is impeded on the desert slope
Upon his way, that he has turned through terror,
And I fear, may be so lost,
That I am too late to save him,
From what I have heard in Heaven.

Go to him now, and with your ornate words,
Give him what he needs to be free,

Assist him so, that I may be consoled.

Beatrice am I, who do bid thee go;
I come from there, where I would fain return;
Love moved me, which compelleth me to speak.
When I shall be in presence of my Lord,
Full often will I praise thee unto him.'
Then paused she, and thereafter I began:

'O Lady of virtue, thou alone through whom
The human race exceedeth all contained
Within the heaven that has the lesser circles,

So grateful unto me is thy commandment,
To obey, if 'twere already done, were late;
No farther need'st thou ope to me thy wish.

But the cause tell me why thou dost not shun
The here descending down into this centre,
From the vast place thou burnest to return to.'

'Since thou wouldst fain so inwardly discern,
Briefly will I relate,' she answered me,
'Why I am not afraid to enter here.

Of those things only should one be afraid
Which have the power of doing others harm;
Of the rest, no; because they are not fearful.

God in his mercy such created me
That misery of yours attains me not,
Nor any flame assails me of this burning.

A gentle Lady is in Heaven, who grieves
At this impediment, to which I send thee,
So that stern judgment there above is broken.

In her entreaty she besought Lucia,
And said, "Thy faithful one now stands in need
Of thee, and unto thee I recommend him."

Lucia, foe of all that cruel is,
Hastened away, and came unto the place
Where I was sitting with the ancient Rachel.

"Beatrice" said she, "the true praise of God.
Why succourest thou not him, who loved thee so,
For thee he issued from the vulgar herd?

And assist him, so I may be at ease.

I am Beatrice, who asks this of you;
I come from there, where I would return;
Love moved me and compelled me to speak.
When I am in the presence of my Lord,
I will praise you to him.'
Then she paused and I began:

'Oh, Lady of virtue, through whom
The human race holds higher
Than the heaven with less circles,

I would be glad to obey your command,
Even if it is too late;
Just tell me what you wish.

But tell me why you are not afraid
To descend down into this place,
From where you long to return.'

'Since you want to know,
I will tell you briefly,' she answered,
'Why I am not afraid to enter here.

One should only be afraid of those things
That have the power of doing others harm;
And nothing else.

In his divine mercy, God made me in such a way
You cannot quite understand,
That even the flames do not burn me.

A gentle Lady in Heaven, grieves
At this journey on which I send you,
So that she broke her own best judgment.

She summoned Lucia,
And said, "Your faithful one stands in need
Of you and I command you to help him."

Lucia, enemy to all that is cruel,
Hastened away and came to the place
Where I was sitting with the ancient Rachel.

"Beatrice" she said, "By the true praise of God,
Why have you not saved him, who loved you so,
When he called out to you?

Dost thou not hear the pity of his plaint? Dost thou not see the death that combats him Beside that flood, where ocean has no vaunt?"	*Didn't you hear the pity in his cry?* *Did you not see the death surrounding him?* *On that river like an ocean?"*
Never were persons in the world so swift To work their weal and to escape their woe, As I, after such words as these were uttered, Came hither downward from my blessed seat, Confiding in thy dignified discourse, Which honours thee, and those who've listened to it.'	*No one in the world moved as quickly as I,* *To work and escape their woe,* *After these words were uttered,* *I came down from my blessed seat,* *Telling you of my plan,* *To bring you honor and anyone who listens.'*
After she thus had spoken unto me, Weeping, her shining eyes she turned away; Whereby she made me swifter in my coming;	*After she said this to me,* *She turned away crying,* *Which made me come faster;*
And unto thee I came, as she desired; I have delivered thee from that wild beast, Which barred the beautiful mountain's short ascent.	*So, here I am, as she desired;* *I have saved you from the wild beast,* *Which barred the beautiful mountain's short ascent.*
What is it, then? Why, why dost thou delay? Why is such baseness bedded in thy heart? Daring and hardihood why hast thou not,	*What is it, then? Why are you delaying?* *Why is fear embedded in your heart?* *You should be overcome with bravery,*
Seeing that three such Ladies benedight Are caring for thee in the court of Heaven, And so much good my speech doth promise thee?"	*Hearing three such Ladies,* *Care for you from Heaven,* *I encourage you to go on.*
Even as the flowerets, by nocturnal chill, Bowed down and closed, when the sun whitens them,	*Like the flowers in winter* *Bow down and close, when the sun takes away their color,*
Uplift themselves all open on their stems;	*Uplift themselves on their stems;*
Such I became with my exhausted strength, And such good courage to my heart there coursed, That I began, like an intrepid person:	*I flew with all my strength,* *With courage coursing through my heart,* *And began to speak:*
"O she compassionate, who succoured me, And courteous thou, who hast obeyed so soon The words of truth which she addressed to thee!	*"Oh compassionate lady who moved me,* *I obey and hear* *The words of truth you speak to me!*
Thou hast my heart so with desire disposed To the adventure, with these words of thine, That to my first intent I have returned.	*You have filled my heart with new desire* *For the adventure, with your words,* *So, I have decided to return to my previous endeavor.*
Now go, for one sole will is in us both, Thou Leader, and thou Lord, and Master thou." Thus said I to him; and when he had moved,	*Now let us go as one soul and one will,* *You are my leader, Lord and Master"* *When I said this and he moved,*

I entered on the deep and savage way.

I entered the deep and savage way.

Inferno: Canto III

"Through me the way is to the city dolent;
Through me the way is to eternal dole;
Through me the way among the people lost.

Justice incited my sublime Creator;
Created me divine Omnipotence,
The highest Wisdom and the primal Love.
Before me there were no created things,
Only eterne, and I eternal last.
All hope abandon, ye who enter in!"

These words in sombre colour I beheld
Written upon the summit of a gate;
Whence I: "Their sense is, Master, hard to me!"

And he to me, as one experienced:
"Here all suspicion needs must be abandoned,
All cowardice must needs be here extinct.

We to the place have come, where I have told thee
Thou shalt behold the people dolorous
Who have foregone the good of intellect."

And after he had laid his hand on mine
With joyful mien, whence I was comforted,
He led me in among the secret things.

There sighs, complaints, and ululations loud
Resounded through the air without a star,
Whence I, at the beginning, wept thereat.

Languages diverse, horrible dialects,
Accents of anger, words of agony,
And voices high and hoarse, with sound of hands,

Made up a tumult that goes whirling on
For ever in that air for ever black,
Even as the sand doth, when the whirlwind breathes.

And I, who had my head with horror bound,
Said: "Master, what is this which now I hear?
What folk is this, which seems by pain so vanquished?"

"I will show you the way to the city of suffering;
I will show you the way to eternal sadness;
I will show you the way of lost people.

My Creator was inspired by justice;
He created me with divine Omnipotence,
The highest Wisdom and the most primal Love.
Before me, nothing was created,
Only eternity and I am eternal.
Abandon all hope, you who enter!"

I beheld these somber words
Written upon the top of a gate;
I said: "I don't understand, Master!"

And he said, as one with experience:
"You must abandon all suspicion and,
All cowardice must be extinguished.

We have come to the place I told you about
You will see suffering people
Who have not used good judgment."

Afterwards he laid his hand on mine
Once I was comforted,
He led me into the land of secret things.

There I heard sighs, complaints, and loud wailings
Resounding through the air,
Where I began to weep.

Diverse languages and horrible dialects,
Accents of anger and words of agony,
High hoarse voices with the sound of hands

Made a whirling tumultuous noise
In that black air,
Like the does in a whirlwind.

In my horror, I
Said: "Master, what is that I hear?
What people are vanquished by such pain?"

And he to me: "This miserable mode
Maintain the melancholy souls of those
Who lived withouten infamy or praise.
Commingled are they with that caitiff choir
Of Angels, who have not rebellious been,
Nor faithful were to God, but were for self.

The heavens expelled them, not to be less fair;
Nor them the nethermore abyss receives,
For glory none the damned would have from them."

And I: "O Master, what so grievous is
To these, that maketh them lament so sore?"
He answered: "I will tell thee very briefly.

These have no longer any hope of death;
And this blind life of theirs is so debased,
They envious are of every other fate.

No fame of them the world permits to be;
Misericord and Justice both disdain them.
Let us not speak of them, but look, and pass."

And I, who looked again, beheld a banner,
Which, whirling round, ran on so rapidly,
That of all pause it seemed to me indignant;

And after it there came so long a train
Of people, that I ne'er would have believed
That ever Death so many had undone.

When some among them I had recognised,
I looked, and I beheld the shade of him
Who made through cowardice the great refusal.

Forthwith I comprehended, and was certain,
That this the sect was of the caitiff wretches
Hateful to God and to his enemies.

These miscreants, who never were alive,
Were naked, and were stung exceedingly
By gadflies and by hornets that were there.

These did their faces irrigate with blood,
Which, with their tears commingled, at their feet
By the disgusting worms was gathered up.

He replied: "This miserable place
Maintains the melancholy souls of those
Who lived without doing good or bad.
They live with a despicable choir
Of Angels, who were neither rebellious
Nor faithful to God, only to themselves.

The heavens expelled them, but not unfairly;
They do not receive the fates of the abyss,
For the damned would not have them."

I said: "Oh Master, what is so grievous
To these that make them lament so sorely?"
He answered: "I will tell you very briefly.

These souls have no hope of death;
Their life is so vile,
They are envious of every other fate.

The world does not permit them any memory;
Misery and Justice overlook them.
Let's not talk about them, but look and pass."

I looked again and saw a banner,
Which was whirling around, moving so rapidly,
Nothing seemed able to stop it.

Running after it was a long train
Of people, I never would have believed
Death would have cheated so many.

I recognized some,
I looked and saw the shadow of one
Who through cowardly actions a great refusal was
born.
Then I understood and was sure,
That this group of damned souls
Hateful to God and his enemies

Were miscreants, who never truly lived.
They were naked and being stung
By flies and hornets.

Their faces gushed with blood,
Combining with their tears, streaming to their feet
Where disgusting worms gathered.

And when to gazing farther I betook me.

People I saw on a great river's bank;
Whence said I: "Master, now vouchsafe to me,
That I may know who these are, and what law
Makes them appear so ready to pass over,

As I discern athwart the dusky light."

And he to me: "These things shall all be known
To thee, as soon as we our footsteps stay
Upon the dismal shore of Acheron."

Then with mine eyes ashamed and downward cast,
Fearing my words might irksome be to him,
From speech refrained I till we reached the river.

And lo! towards us coming in a boat
An old man, hoary with the hair of eld,
Crying: "Woe unto you, ye souls depraved!

Hope nevermore to look upon the heavens;
I come to lead you to the other shore,
To the eternal shades in heat and frost.

And thou, that yonder standest, living soul,
Withdraw thee from these people, who are dead!"
But when he saw that I did not withdraw,

He said: "By other ways, by other ports
Thou to the shore shalt come, not here, for passage;

A lighter vessel needs must carry thee."

And unto him the Guide: "Vex thee not, Charon;
It is so willed there where is power to do
That which is willed; and farther question not."

Thereat were quieted the fleecy cheeks
Of him the ferryman of the livid fen,
Who round about his eyes had wheels of flame.

But all those souls who weary were and naked
Their colour changed and gnashed their teeth together,
As soon as they had heard those cruel words.

God they blasphemed and their progenitors,
The human race, the place, the time, the seed
Of their engendering and of their birth!

Gazing further I saw
People on a great river's bank;
I said: "Master, now tell me truly,
So, I may know who they are, and what law
Makes them appear so ready to pass over,

As I see them standing side-by-side in the dim
light."
Virgil said: "You will know all of these things
As soon as we step upon
The dismal shore of Acheron."

Then in shame, with downward cast eyes,
Fearing my words might be bothersome,
I refrained from speaking until we reached the
river.
To my surprise a boat came towards us
Driven by an old man with gray hair,
Crying: "Pity upon you depraved souls!

Do not ever again hope to look upon the heavens;
I come to lead you to the other shore,
To an eternal heat and frost.

And you standing there, living soul,
Get away from these dead people!"
But, when he saw I did not move,

He said: "There are other ways and ports
You may come to the shore, but you cannot use
this passage;
A lighter vessel must carry you."

The Guide said to him: "Don't worry Charon;
It is willed by a higher power
So don't question."

This quieted the hairy cheeks
Of the ferryman of the gray marsh,
Who had fire burning in his eyes.

But all those souls who were weary and naked
Gnashed their teeth as their color changed,
As soon as they heard these cruel words.

They blasphemed God and their ancestors,
The human race, the place, the time, the moment
Of their conception and of their birth!

Thereafter all together they drew back,
Bitterly weeping, to the accursed shore,
Which waiteth every man who fears not God.

Charon the demon, with the eyes of glede,
Beckoning to them, collects them all together,
Beats with his oar whoever lags behind.
As in the autumn-time the leaves fall off,
First one and then another, till the branch
Unto the earth surrenders all its spoils;

In similar wise the evil seed of Adam
Throw themselves from that margin one by one,
At signals, as a bird unto its lure.

So they depart across the dusky wave,
And ere upon the other side they land,
Again on this side a new troop assembles.

"My son," the courteous Master said to me,
"All those who perish in the wrath of God
Here meet together out of every land;

And ready are they to pass o'er the river,
Because celestial Justice spurs them on,
So that their fear is turned into desire.

This way there never passes a good soul;
And hence if Charon doth complain of thee,
Well mayst thou know now what his speech imports."

This being finished, all the dusk champaign
Trembled so violently, that of that terror
The recollection bathes me still with sweat.

The land of tears gave forth a blast of wind,
And fulminated a vermilion light,
Which overmastered in me every sense,

And as a man whom sleep hath seized I fell.

Afterwards, they drew back together,
Weeping bitterly to the accursed shore,
Which wits for every man who doesn't fear God.

Charon the demon with red eyes,
Beckoning to them, collected them together
And beat anyone who lagged behind with his oar.
As in the Fall when the leaves drop,
First one and then another, until the branch
Surrenders all to the earth;

Like the evil children of Adam
Throwing themselves from the edge one by one,
As a bird flying into a trap.

They departed across the dark wave,
And once upon the other side,
A new group assembled.

"My son," the polite Master said to me,
"All who perish by God's wrath
Meet together here from around the world;

To pass over the river,
Because celestial Justice spurs them on,
So their fear is transformed into desire.

This way, a good soul never passes;
And so, if Charon complains about you,
Well you must know why."

With this, the earth
Trembled so violently, that remembering the terror
Bathes me still with sweat.

The land of tears gave a blast of wind,
And cast green light,
Which overwhelmed my every sense,

And like a man taken by sleep, I fainted.

Inferno: Canto IV

Broke the deep lethargy within my head A heavy thunder, so that I upstarted, Like to a person who by force is wakened;	*The deep sleep was broken* *By a loud clap of thunder and* *Like a person who is awakened by force I jumped;*
And round about I moved my rested eyes, Uprisen erect, and steadfastly I gazed, To recognise the place wherein I was.	*And looking around with rested eyes,* *I stood and tried,* *To recognize the place where I was.*
True is it, that upon the verge I found me Of the abysmal valley dolorous, That gathers thunder of infinite ululations.	*I found myself* *In the abysmal valley of the suffering* *That holds the infinite wails of the damned.*
Obscure, profound it was, and nebulous, So that by fixing on its depths my sight Nothing whatever I discerned therein.	*It was obscure and cloudy,* *So I fixed my eyes on its depths* *And could not make out anything within.*
"Let us descend now into the blind world," Began the Poet, pallid utterly; "I will be first, and thou shalt second be."	*"Let's descend now into the blind world,"* *The Poet began,* *"I will go first, and you second."*
And I, who of his colour was aware, Said: "How shall I come, if thou art afraid, Who'rt wont to be a comfort to my fears?"	*I, unaware of my color,* *Said: "How can I come, if you are afraid,* *The person who is supposed to be a comfort to* *me?"*
And he to me: "The anguish of the people Who are below here in my face depicts That pity which for terror thou hast taken.	*He replied: "The anguish of the people* *Who are below here I do not fear.* *What you mistake for fear is pity.*
Let us go on, for the long way impels us." Thus he went in, and thus he made me enter The foremost circle that surrounds the abyss.	*Let's go on, for we have a long way."* *Thus, he went in and I followed* *Into the first circle that surrounds the abyss.*
There, as it seemed to me from listening, Were lamentations none, but only sighs, That tremble made the everlasting air.	*From what I heard,* *There were no lamentations, only sighs,* *That trembled the eternal air.*
And this arose from sorrow without torment, Which the crowds had, that many were and great, Of infants and of women and of men.	*This sound was born from sorrow without torment,* *From the crowds of great,* *Of infants, women and men.*
To me the Master good: "Thou dost not ask What spirits these, which thou beholdest, are?	*The Master said: "You do not ask* *What spirits these are, which you see?*

Now will I have thee know, ere thou go farther,	*I will tell you before you go farther,*
That they sinned not; and if they merit had,	*They were not sinners; and if they had merit*
'Tis not enough, because they had not baptism	*It was not enough, because they were not baptized*
Which is the portal of the Faith thou holdest;	*Which is the way to salvation according to your Faith;*
And if they were before Christianity,	*And if they lived before Christianity,*
In the right manner they adored not God;	*And they did not adore God;*
And among such as these am I myself.	*Including myself.*
For such defects, and not for other guilt,	*Because of this and nothing else,*
Lost are we and are only so far punished,	*We are lost but not punished,*
That without hope we live on in desire."	*So we live without hope in constant desire."*
Great grief seized on my heart when this I heard,	*I was overcome with grief when I heard this,*
Because some people of much worthiness	*Because some worthy people*
I knew, who in that Limbo were suspended.	*I knew, were in that place of Limbo.*
"Tell me, my Master, tell me, thou my Lord,"	*"Tell me, my Master, tell me, my Lord,"*
Began I, with desire of being certain	*I said, wanting to be sure*
Of that Faith which o'ercometh every error,	*Of the Faith which overcomes every error,*
"Came any one by his own merit hence,	*"Has anyone been released by his own merit,*
Or by another's, who was blessed thereafter?"	*Or by another's?"*
And he, who understood my covert speech,	*And understanding my question,*
Replied: "I was a novice in this state,	*He replied: "I was a novice in this state,*
When I saw hither come a Mighty One,	*When I saw a Mighty One,*
With sign of victory incoronate.	*With a sign of victory.*
Hence he drew forth the shade of the First Parent,	*He withdrew the First Parent,*
And that of his son Abel, and of Noah,	*And his son, Abel, and Noah,*
Of Moses the lawgiver, and the obedient	*He took Moses, the lawgiver, and the obedient*
Abraham, patriarch, and David, king,	*Patriarchal Abraham, and King David,*
Israel with his father and his children,	*Israel with his father and his children,*
And Rachel, for whose sake he did so much,	*And Rachel for whose sake he did so much,*
And others many, and he made them blessed;	*And he blessed many others;*
And thou must know, that earlier than these	*You must know that anyone as old as these*
Never were any human spirits saved."	*Were never saved spirits."*
We ceased not to advance because he spake,	*We stopped while he spoke,*
But still were passing onward through the forest,	*But still passed through the forest*
The forest, say I, of thick-crowded ghosts.	*Of crowded ghosts.*
Not very far as yet our way had gone	*When we had not gone very far*
This side the summit, when I saw a fire	*I saw a fire on this side of the summit,*

That overcame a hemisphere of darkness.

We were a little distant from it still,
But not so far that I in part discerned not
That honourable people held that place.

"O thou who honourest every art and science,

Who may these be, which such great honour have,
That from the fashion of the rest it parts them?"

And he to me: "The honourable name,
That sounds of them above there in thy life,
Wins grace in Heaven, that so advances them."

In the mean time a voice was heard by me:
"All honour be to the pre-eminent Poet;
His shade returns again, that was departed."

After the voice had ceased and quiet was,
Four mighty shades I saw approaching us;
Semblance had they nor sorrowful nor glad.

To say to me began my gracious Master:
"Him with that falchion in his hand behold,
Who comes before the three, even as their lord.

That one is Homer, Poet sovereign;
He who comes next is Horace, the satirist;
The third is Ovid, and the last is Lucan.

Because to each of these with me applies

The name that solitary voice proclaimed,
They do me honour, and in that do well."

Thus I beheld assemble the fair school
Of that lord of the song pre-eminent,
Who o'er the others like an eagle soars.

When they together had discoursed somewhat,
They turned to me with signs of salutation,
And on beholding this, my Master smiled;

And more of honour still, much more, they did me,
In that they made me one of their own band;
So that the sixth was I, 'mid so much wit.

That overcame the darkness.

We were a good distance from it,
But I still discerned
That honorable people were in that place.

"Oh, those who are known in every art and science,
Hasn't there honor
Set them apart from the rest?

He said: "The honorable name
That they were known by in life,
Wins grace in Heaven, so advancing them."

In the meantime, I heard a voice nearby:
"All honor be to the pre-eminent Poet;
His soul returns."

After the voice ceased,
Four mighty shadows approached us;
Showing no signs of sorrow or happiness.

My gracious Master said to me:
"Look at him with that sword in his hand,
Who walks before the other three as their lord.

That is the sovereign Poet, Homer.
Next is the satirist, Horace;
And the third is Ovid, followed by Lucan.

Because each of these honor me with their presence
And call me by that name,
They honor me well.

I saw the group of fair souls
Of that lord of the first song,
Who soared over the others like an eagle.

When they came closer,
They turned to me with greetings,
And seeing this, my Master smiled;

They honored me,
In that they accepted me into their group,
Making me the sixth among the intelligent souls.

Thus we went on as far as to the light, Things saying 'tis becoming to keep silent, As was the saying of them where I was.	*Together we went on as far as to the light,* *Saying it is more becoming to keep quiet,* *As was their motto there.*
We came unto a noble castle's foot, Seven times encompassed with lofty walls, Defended round by a fair rivulet;	*We came to the bottom of a noble castle,* *Surrounded by seven high walls,* *And encircled by a defending river;*
This we passed over even as firm ground; Through portals seven I entered with these Sages; We came into a meadow of fresh verdure.	*We passed over the river as if it were firm ground;* *I entered one of seven doors with these sages;* *We came into a fresh green meadow.*
People were there with solemn eyes and slow, Of great authority in their countenance; They spake but seldom, and with gentle voices.	*People were there with solemn, slow eyes,* *They looked to have great authority;* *They spoke very little with gentle voices.*
Thus we withdrew ourselves upon one side Into an opening luminous and lofty, So that they all of them were visible.	*We went to one side* *Into a luminous, lofty opening,* *So that they were all visible.*
There opposite, upon the green enamel, Were pointed out to me the mighty spirits, Whom to have seen I feel myself exalted.	*Opposite the green enamel,* *The mighty spirits were pointed out to me,* *And I was honored to behold.*
I saw Electra with companions many, 'Mongst whom I knew both Hector and Aeneas, Caesar in armour with gerfalcon eyes;	*I saw Electra with many companions,* *Amongst whom I knew Hector and Aeneas;* *Caesar with his greedy eyes was in armor.*
I saw Camilla and Penthesilea On the other side, and saw the King Latinus, Who with Lavinia his daughter sat;	*I saw Camilla and Penthesilea* *On the other side, and King Latinus,* *Who sat with his daughter Lavinia.*
I saw that Brutus who drove Tarquin forth, Lucretia, Julia, Marcia, and Cornelia, And saw alone, apart, the Saladin.	*I saw Brutus who drove forth Tarquin,* *Lucretia, Julia, Marcia, and Cornelia,* *And sitting alone apart from the rest, Saladin.*
When I had lifted up my brows a little, The Master I beheld of those who know, Sit with his philosophic family.	*When I had lifted my brow a little,* *I saw the Master of those souls,* *Sitting with his philosophic family.*
All gaze upon him, and all do him honour. There I beheld both Socrates and Plato, Who nearer him before the others stand;	*Everyone gazed upon him, honoring him.* *There I beheld both Socrates and Plato,* *Who stood near him before the others.*
Democritus, who puts the world on chance, Diogenes, Anaxagoras, and Thales, Zeno, Empedocles, and Heraclitus;	*Democritus, who put the world on chance,* *Dogenes, Anaxagoras, and Thales,* *Zeno, Empedocles, and Heraclitus;*

Of qualities I saw the good collector,
Hight Dioscorides; and Orpheus saw I,
Tully and Livy, and moral Seneca,

Euclid, geometrician, and Ptolemy,
Galen, Hippocrates, and Avicenna,
Averroes, who the great Comment made.

I cannot all of them pourtray in full,
Because so drives me onward the long theme,
That many times the word comes short of fact.

The sixfold company in two divides;
Another way my sapient Guide conducts me
Forth from the quiet to the air that trembles;

And to a place I come where nothing shines.

I also saw the good collector,
High Dioscorides and Orpheus,
Tully, Livy and the moral Seneca,

Euclid, the mathematician, and Ptolemy,
Galen, Hippocrates, and Avicenna,
Averroes, who made the great Comment.

I cannot portray them fully,
Because the list of attributes is so long,
That I am short of words.

The company of six divided in tow,
My Guide conducted me
Forth from the quiet to the trembling air;

And to a place where nothing shined.

Inferno: Canto V

Thus I descended out of the first circle Down to the second, that less space begirds, And so much greater dole, that goads to wailing	*I then descended out of the first circle* *Going down to the second which was smaller* *And with much greater torment, giving way to* *wailing.*
There standeth Minos horribly, and snarls; Examines the transgressions at the entrance;	*There stood horrible Minos snarling;* *And examining the transgressions of the damned* *at theentrance;*
Judges, and sends according as he girds him.	*He stood as judge and condemned the souls* *accordingly.*
I say, that when the spirit evil-born Cometh before him, wholly it confesses; And this discriminator of transgressions	*When the evil spirit* *Came before him and confessed;* *This discriminator of transgressions*
Seeth what place in Hell is meet for it; Girds himself with his tail as many times As grades he wishes it should be thrust down.	*Saw what place in Hell was appropriate;* *He encircled himself with his tail that many times* *To indicate what circle of Hell the soul was sent.*
Always before him many of them stand; They go by turns each one unto the judgment; They speak, and hear, and then are downward hurled.	*Many of them stood before him;* *Taking turns to be judged;* *They spoke, listened, and were then hurled* *downward.*
"O thou, that to this dolorous hostelry	*"Hey, come here, you who enter the place of* *suffering,"*
Comest," said Minos to me, when he saw me, Leaving the practice of so great an office,	*Said Minos to me, when he saw me,* *Not partaking in the practice,*
"Look how thou enterest, and in whom thou trustest; Let not the portal's amplitude deceive thee." And unto him my Guide: "Why criest thou too?	*"Look how you enter and who you trust;* *Don't let the vastness of this place fool you."* *To him, my Guide responded: "Why are you* *crying, too?*
Do not impede his journey fate-ordained; It is so willed there where is power to do That which is willed; and ask no further question."	*Do not impede his journey that fate ordained;* *The power has willed it,* *So ask no other questions."*
And now begin the dolesome notes to grow Audible unto me; now am I come There where much lamentation strikes upon me.	*The sad sounds began to grow* *Audible to me, as I came* *To the place of overwhelming sadness.*
I came into a place mute of all light, Which bellows as the sea does in a tempest, If by opposing winds 't is combated.	*I came to a place without any light,* *As scary as a raging sea,* *Combating opposing winds.*

The infernal hurricane that never rests
Hurtles the spirits onward in its rapine;
Whirling them round, and smiting, it molests them.

When they arrive before the precipice,
There are the shrieks, the plaints, and the laments,
There they blaspheme the puissance divine.

I understood that unto such a torment
The carnal malefactors were condemned,
Who reason subjugate to appetite.

And as the wings of starlings bear them on
In the cold season in large band and full,
So doth that blast the spirits maledict;

It hither, thither, downward, upward, drives them;
No hope doth comfort them for evermore,
Not of repose, but even of lesser pain.

And as the cranes go chanting forth their lays,
Making in air a long line of themselves,
So saw I coming, uttering lamentations,

Shadows borne onward by the aforesaid stress.
Whereupon said I: "Master, who are those
People, whom the black air so castigates?"

"The first of those, of whom intelligence
Thou fain wouldst have," then said he unto me,
"The empress was of many languages.

To sensual vices she was so abandoned,
That lustful she made licit in her law,
To remove the blame to which she had been led.

She is Semiramis, of whom we read
That she succeeded Ninus, and was his spouse;
She held the land which now the Sultan rules.

The next is she who killed herself for love,
And broke faith with the ashes of Sichaeus;
Then Cleopatra the voluptuous."

Helen I saw, for whom so many ruthless
Seasons revolved; and saw the great Achilles,
Who at the last hour combated with Love.

The burning hurricane that never rests
Hurtled the spirits onward by force;
Whirling them around and smiting them.

When they arrived before the precipice,
The place of shrieks, plaints, and laments,
They blasphemed the divine power.

I understood the torment and
Condemned the carnal malefactors,
Who are controlled by appetite.

And as the wings of starlings carried them onward
In the cold season in full flocks,
The spirits were cursed;

It drove them up and down, side-to-side;
No hope comforted them,
In their repose or pain

And like cranes going forward chanting,
And flying in long lines,
I saw them coming, uttering lamentations,

Shadows urged onward by great stress.
I asked the Master: "Who are those
People, punished by the black air?"

"The first of those, whose intelligence
You would gladly have," he said to me,
"The empress knew many languages.

She abandoned sensual vices,
And made lust lawful,
To remove her own blame.

She is Semiramis, of whom we have read
That succeeded Ninus, and was his wife;
She held the land now ruled by Sultan.

The next is she who killed herself for love,
And broke faith with the ashes of Sichaeus;
Then there is Cleopatra the voluptuous."

I saw Helen, for whom so many ruthless
Seasons revolved; and the great Achilles,
Who at the last hour combated with Love.

Paris I saw, Tristan; and more than a thousand Shades did he name and point out with his finger, Whom Love had separated from our life.	*I saw Paris, Tristan, and a thousand more* *He named and pointed out,* *Whom Love had separated from life.*
After that I had listened to my Teacher, Naming the dames of eld and cavaliers, Pity prevailed, and I was nigh bewildered.	*After I had listened to my Teacher,* *Naming the dames and cavaliers of long ago,* *I was overcome with pity and bewilderment.*
And I began: "O Poet, willingly Speak would I to those two, who go together, And seem upon the wind to be so light."	*I began: "Oh Poet, Tell me,* *Who are the two going together,* *Seeming so light upon the wind."*
And, he to me: "Thou'lt mark, when they shall be Nearer to us; and then do thou implore them By love which leadeth them, and they will come."	*He told me: "You will know, when they are* *Nearer to us; Implore them* *With love which leads them, and they will come."*
Soon as the wind in our direction sways them, My voice uplift I: "O ye weary souls!	*As soon as the wind blew them in our direction,* *I uplifted my voice and said: "Oh you weary* *souls!*
Come speak to us, if no one interdicts it."	*Come speak to us if no one opposes it."*
As turtle-doves, called onward by desire, With open and steady wings to the sweet nest Fly through the air by their volition borne,	*Like turtle doves, called onward by desire,* *With open and steady wings* *Flying through the air instinctively to their home,*
So came they from the band where Dido is, Approaching us athwart the air malign, So strong was the affectionate appeal.	*They came from the group of Dido* *Approaching us through the malignant air,* *Looking quite appealing.*
"O living creature gracious and benignant, Who visiting goest through the purple air Us, who have stained the world incarnadine,	*"Oh living creature, gracious and benign,* *Who goes through the purple air to visit,* *Us, who have stained the world blood red,*
If were the King of the Universe our friend, We would pray unto him to give thee peace, Since thou hast pity on our woe perverse.	*If the King of the Universe was our friend,* *We would pray to him to grant you peace,* *Since you have pity on our perverse* *circumstances.*
Of what it pleases thee to hear and speak, That will we hear, and we will speak to you, While silent is the wind, as it is now.	*Whatever you wish to hear or say,* *We will listen or speak* *While the wind is silent as it is now.*
Sitteth the city, wherein I was born, Upon the sea-shore where the Po descends To rest in peace with all his retinue.	*The city where I was born sits,* *Upon the seashore where the Po descends* *To rest in peace with all of its attendees.*
Love, that on gentle heart doth swiftly seize, Seized this man for the person beautiful That was ta'en from me, and still the mode offends me.	*Love, that swiftly seizes the gentle heart,* *Seized this man for the beautiful person* *That was taken from me and still offends me.*

Love, that exempts no one beloved from loving,
Seized me with pleasure of this man so strongly,
That, as thou seest, it doth not yet desert me;

Love has conducted us unto one death;
Caina waiteth him who quenched our life!"
These words were borne along from them to us.
As soon as I had heard those souls tormented,
I bowed my face, and so long held it down
Until the Poet said to me: "What thinkest?"

When I made answer, I began: "Alas!
How many pleasant thoughts, how much desire,
Conducted these unto the dolorous pass!"

Then unto them I turned me, and I spake,
And I began: "Thine agonies, Francesca,
Sad and compassionate to weeping make me.

But tell me, at the time of those sweet sighs,
By what and in what manner Love conceded,
That you should know your dubious desires?"

And she to me: "There is no greater sorrow
Than to be mindful of the happy time
In misery, and that thy Teacher knows.

But, if to recognise the earliest root
Of love in us thou hast so great desire,
I will do even as he who weeps and speaks.

One day we reading were for our delight
Of Launcelot, how Love did him enthral.
Alone we were and without any fear.

Full many a time our eyes together drew
That reading, and drove the colour from our faces;
But one point only was it that o'ercame us.

When as we read of the much-longed-for smile
Being by such a noble lover kissed,
This one, who ne'er from me shall be divided,

Kissed me upon the mouth all palpitating.
Galeotto was the book and he who wrote it.
That day no farther did we read therein."

Love, that hides from no one,
Seized me with desire for this man, so strongly,
You may still see it;

Love, that has brought us to one death;
Caina waits for him who took our lives!"
These words were said to us.
As soon as I heard these poor tormented souls,
I bowed my face, and held it down
Until the Poet said: "What are you thinking?"

When I could speak, I said: "Alas!
How many pleasant thoughts, how much desire,
Brought them to this suffering!"

Then to them I said,
"Your agonies, Francesca
Make me weep with compassion.

But tell me, at the time of those sweet moments,
Conceded in Love, what and how
Did you know your dubious desires?"

She responded: "There is no greater sorrow
Than to remember the happy times
In misery, and that your Teacher knows.

But, if I recognize the beginning
Of our love affair,
I will weep, also.

One day we were reading for some fun
Of Lancelot and how love enthralled him.
We were alone and without any fear.

Many times our eyes drew together
Reading and drained the color from our faces;
So at one point love overcame us.

When we read of the much-longed-for smile
I was by such a noble lover, I kissed
Him, who never will be apart from me,

He kissed me upon my palpitating mouth.
The book and its author were so gallant.
We did not read it anymore."

And all the while one spirit uttered this,
The other one did weep so, that, for pity,
I swooned away as if I had been dying,

And fell, even as a dead body falls.

While the one spirit uttered this,
The other wept so pitifully,
I swooned away as if I was dying,

And fell like a dead body.

Inferno: Canto VI

At the return of consciousness, that closed
Before the pity of those two relations,
Which utterly with sadness had confused me,

New torments I behold, and new tormented
Around me, whichsoever way I move,
And whichsoever way I turn, and gaze.

In the third circle am I of the rain
Eternal, maledict, and cold, and heavy;
Its law and quality are never new.

Huge hail, and water sombre-hued, and snow,
Athwart the tenebrous air pour down amain;
Noisome the earth is, that receiveth this.

Cerberus, monster cruel and uncouth,
With his three gullets like a dog is barking
Over the people that are there submerged.

Red eyes he has, and unctuous beard and black,
And belly large, and armed with claws his hands;

He rends the spirits, flays, and quarters them.

Howl the rain maketh them like unto dogs;
One side they make a shelter for the other;
Oft turn themselves the wretched reprobates.

When Cerberus perceived us, the great worm!
His mouths he opened, and displayed his tusks;
Not a limb had he that was motionless.

And my Conductor, with his spans extended,
Took of the earth, and with his fists well filled,
He threw it into those rapacious gullets.

Such as that dog is, who by barking craves,
And quiet grows soon as his food he gnaws,
For to devour it he but thinks and struggles,

The like became those muzzles filth-begrimed

At the return of consciousness I lost,
After seeing the pity of those two souls,
Which filled me with sadness and confusion,

I beheld now torments, and newly tormented
Around me, wherever I moved,
And wherever I looked.

I was in the third circle filled with eternal rain,
And cold, heavy suffering,
Its law and quality never changing.

Huge hail, murky water, and snow
Poured from the tenebrous air;
Making the earth below noisy.

The cruel and uncouth monster, Cerberus,
With his three heads barking like a dog
Submerged over the people there.

He had red eyes and an unctuous, black beard,
And large belly. His hands were armed with
claws;
He flayed the spirits into quarters.

The howling rains made them like dogs;
One side making shelter for the other;
The wretched turning themselves.

When Cerberus, the great worm, perceived us!
His mouth opened displaying tusks;
His limbs flailing in constant motion.

My Conductor, with his arms extended,
Took fists full of dirt,
And threw it into those enormous mouths.

Like a barking dog that craves food,
The quiet grew as he gnawed,
Trying to devour it.

His muzzle becoming filthy,

Of Cerberus the demon, who so thunders
Over the souls that they would fain be deaf.

We passed across the shadows, which subdues
The heavy rain-storm, and we placed our feet
Upon their vanity that person seems.

They all were lying prone upon the earth,
Excepting one, who sat upright as soon
As he beheld us passing on before him.

"O thou that art conducted through this Hell,"
He said to me, "recall me, if thou canst;
Thyself wast made before I was unmade."

And I to him: "The anguish which thou hast
Perhaps doth draw thee out of my remembrance,
So that it seems not I have ever seen thee.

But tell me who thou art, that in so doleful
A place art put, and in such punishment,
If some are greater, none is so displeasing."

And he to me: "Thy city, which is full
Of envy so that now the sack runs over,
Held me within it in the life serene.

You citizens were wont to call me Ciacco;
For the pernicious sin of gluttony
I, as thou seest, am battered by this rain.

And I, sad soul, am not the only one,
For all these suffer the like penalty
For the like sin;" and word no more spake he.

I answered him: "Ciacco, thy wretchedness
Weighs on me so that it to weep invites me;
But tell me, if thou knowest, to what shall come

The citizens of the divided city;
If any there be just; and the occasion
Tell me why so much discord has assailed it."

And he to me: "They, after long contention,
Will come to bloodshed; and the rustic party
Will drive the other out with much offence.

Then afterwards behoves it this one fall

Cerberus, the demon, thundered
Over the souls that would rather be deaf.

We passed across the shadows, which subdue
The heavy storm, and placed our feet
Upon their earth.

They all were lying prostrate on the ground,
Except one, who sat upright as soon
As he saw us passing on before him.

"Oh you that are led through this Hell,"
He said to me, "Recall me, if you can;
You were alive before I died."

I returned: "The anguish which you have
Keeps me from remembering you,
So I don't know who you are.

But tell me who you are, put in this sorrowful
Place, and in such punishment, so that
If some are greater, none can be so awful."

He said to me: "Your city, which is full,
Of envy so that it runs over,
Held me in life.

The citizens called me Ciacco;
For the sin of gluttony,
I am now battered by this rain.

And I am not the only one,
For all these suffer the same penalty
For similar sins;" He stopped speaking.

I answered him: "Ciacco, your wretchedness
Weighs on me and makes me want to weep;
But tell me, if you know, what will happen

To the citizens of the divided city;
If any there are just, tell me why
There is so much discord."

He said, "After long contention, they
Will come to bloodshed; and the older party
Will drive out the other with much offence.

Then afterwards the one who fell,

Within three suns, and rise again the other
By force of him who now is on the coast.

High will it hold its forehead a long while,
Keeping the other under heavy burdens,
Howe'er it weeps thereat and is indignant.
The just are two, and are not understood there;
Envy and Arrogance and Avarice
Are the three sparks that have all hearts enkindled."

Here ended he his tearful utterance;
And I to him: "I wish thee still to teach me,
And make a gift to me of further speech.

Farinata and Tegghiaio, once so worthy,
Jacopo Rusticucci, Arrigo, and Mosca,
And others who on good deeds set their thoughts,

Say where they are, and cause that I may know them;
For great desire constraineth me to learn
If Heaven doth sweeten them, or Hell envenom."

And he: "They are among the blacker souls;
A different sin downweighs them to the bottom;
If thou so far descendest, thou canst see them.

But when thou art again in the sweet world,
I pray thee to the mind of others bring me;
No more I tell thee and no more I answer."

Then his straightforward eyes he turned askance,
Eyed me a little, and then bowed his head;
He fell therewith prone like the other blind.

And the Guide said to me: "He wakes no more
This side the sound of the angelic trumpet;
When shall approach the hostile Potentate,

Each one shall find again his dismal tomb,
Shall reassume his flesh and his own figure,
Shall hear what through eternity re-echoes."

So we passed onward o'er the filthy mixture
Of shadows and of rain with footsteps slow,
Touching a little on the future life.

Wherefore I said: "Master, these torments here,
Will they increase after the mighty sentence,

Within three suns, will rise again and the other
By force who are now on the coast,

Will hold its forehead high for awhile;
Keeping the other under a heavy load
However it cries at that place and is angry
The just are two, and cannot be understood
Envy, Arrogance, and Avarice
Will enkindle their hearts."

He ended his tearful reverie;
And I said: "I wish you would still teach me,
With the gift of further talk.

Farinata and Tegghiaio, once so worthy,
Jacopo Rusticucci, Arrigo, and Mosca,
Set their thoughts on good deeds,

Tell me where they are, because I may know them;
And I want to know
If Heaven sweetens them or Hell devours them."

And he: "They are among the blacker souls;
A different sin holds them at the bottom;
If you descend that far, you can see them.

But when you are in the sweet world again,
I pray you will remind others of me;
That is all I can tell you."

Then he turned his eyes away,
Looked at me a little and bowed his head;
He fell prostrate like the blind others.

The Guide said: "He will not wake any more
This side of the angelic trumpet;
When you approach the hostile Potentate,

Each one will find his dismal tomb again,
Reassuming his own flesh and figure, and
Will hear the echoing of eternity again."

So we passed over the filthy mixture
Of shadows and rain with slow footsteps,
Touching a little on future life.

Then I said: "Master, these torments here,
Will they increase after the mighty sentencing,

Or lesser be, or will they be as burning?"

And he to me: "Return unto thy science,
Which wills, that as the thing more perfect is,
The more it feels of pleasure and of pain.

Albeit that this people maledict
To true perfection never can attain,
Hereafter more than now they look to be."

Round in a circle by that road we went,
Speaking much more, which I do not repeat;
We came unto the point where the descent is;

There we found Plutus the great enemy.

Be lessened, or stay the same?"

He said: "Think about your knowledge of science,
Which states, that as a thing is more perfect,
The more pleasure and pain it feels.

However, these suffering people
Can never attain true perfection,
Any more than they look now to be."

We went around a circle along a road,
Talking as we walked, which I do not repeat;
We came to the point of descent;

There we found Pluto, the great enemy.

Inferno: Canto VII

"Pape Satan, Pape Satan, Aleppe!"
Thus Plutus with his clucking voice began;
And that benignant Sage, who all things knew,

Said, to encourage me: "Let not thy fear
Harm thee; for any power that he may have
Shall not prevent thy going down this crag."

Then he turned round unto that bloated lip,
And said: "Be silent, thou accursed wolf;
Consume within thyself with thine own rage.

Not causeless is this journey to the abyss;
Thus is it willed on high, where Michael wrought
Vengeance upon the proud adultery."

Even as the sails inflated by the wind
Involved together fall when snaps the mast,
So fell the cruel monster to the earth.

Thus we descended into the fourth chasm,
Gaining still farther on the dolesome shore
Which all the woe of the universe insacks.

Justice of God, ah! who heaps up so many
New toils and sufferings as I beheld?
And why doth our transgression waste us so?

As doth the billow there upon Charybdis,
That breaks itself on that which it encounters,
So here the folk must dance their roundelay.

Here saw I people, more than elsewhere, many,
On one side and the other, with great howls,
Rolling weights forward by main force of chest.

They clashed together, and then at that point
Each one turned backward, rolling retrograde,

Crying, "Why keepest?" and, "Why squanderest thou?"

"Pape Satan, Pape Satan, Aleppe!"
Pluto began, with his clucking voice;
The benign Sage, who knew all things,

Said to encourage me: "Don't let your fear
Harm you; For any power he may have
Will not prevent you from going down into this
crag."
Then he turned towards the bloated mouth,
And said: "Be quiet, you accursed wolf;
Contain your rage within yourself.

This journey to the abyss is not without cause;
And is willed on high, where Michael brought
Vengeance upon the proud adulterers."

Like sails inflated by the wind,
Fall when the mast is snapped,
The cruel monster slipped to the earth.

Therefore, we descended into the fourth chasm,
Gaining farther on the sad shore
Which holds all of the woe in the universe.

Justice of God, ha! Who heaps up many
Toils and sufferings?
Why do our transgressions leave us so wasted?

Like the wind upon Charydis,
Breaks itself on all it encounters,
There the folks endured their punishment.

I saw more people than before,
On one side and the other, howling as they
Rolled weights forward.

They clashed together and then
Turned around and rolled backwards,

Crying, "Why did you keep it?" and "Why did you
squander it?"

Thus they returned along the lurid circle

On either hand unto the opposite point,
Shouting their shameful metre evermore.

Then each, when he arrived there, wheeled about
Through his half-circle to another joust;
And I, who had my heart pierced as it were,

Exclaimed: "My Master, now declare to me
What people these are, and if all were clerks,

These shaven crowns upon the left of us."

And he to me: "All of them were asquint
In intellect in the first life, so much
That there with measure they no spending made.

Clearly enough their voices bark it forth,
Whene'er they reach the two points of the circle,
Where sunders them the opposite defect.

Clerks those were who no hairy covering
Have on the head, and Popes and Cardinals,
In whom doth Avarice practise its excess."

And I: "My Master, among such as these
I ought forsooth to recognise some few,
Who were infected with these maladies."

And he to me: "Vain thought thou entertainest;
The undiscerning life which made them sordid
Now makes them unto all discernment dim.

Forever shall they come to these two buttings;
These from the sepulchre shall rise again

With the fist closed, and these with tresses shorn.

Ill giving and ill keeping the fair world
Have ta'en from them, and placed them in this scuffle;

Whate'er it be, no words adorn I for it.
Now canst thou, Son, behold the transient farce

Of goods that are committed unto Fortune,
For which the human race each other buffet;

Afterwards, they returned around the same lurid circle,
Going to the opposite point,
Shouting their same shameful lament forever.

Then upon arriving, each wheeled about
Through his circle to another fight;
And I, with my pierced heart,

Exclaimed: "Master, tell me
What these people are, and if they were all clergymen,
Those souls to the left of us with the shaven heads.

He replied: "All of them were so asquint
In intellect in their first lives,
That they did not spend anything.

Their voices bark forth clearly,
Whenever they reach the two points of the circle,
Which sends them in the opposite direction.

Those without hair were clergymen,
And Popes and Cardinals,
Who bore greedy practices.

I said: "Master, among these,
I should recognize some,
Who were infected with these maladies."

He responded: "That's a vain thought;
The undiscerning life that made them sordid
Now makes them unknown to all.

They shall forever butt together;
Those from the church and the shaved heads will rise again
With their closed fists.

Ill giving and ill keeping, the fair world
Has taken from them, and placed them in this fight;
Whatever it is, there are no words to describe it.
Now can you, Son, understand this temporary farce
Of goods that are committed to Fortune,
For which the human race fight over;

For all the gold that is beneath the moon,
Or ever has been, of these weary souls
Could never make a single one repose."

"Master," I said to him, "now tell me also
What is this Fortune which thou speakest of,
That has the world's goods so within its clutches?"
And he to me: "O creatures imbecile,
What ignorance is this which doth beset you?
Now will I have thee learn my judgment of her.

He whose omniscience everything transcends
The heavens created, and gave who should guide them,
That every part to every part may shine,

Distributing the light in equal measure;
He in like manner to the mundane splendours
Ordained a general ministress and guide,

That she might change at times the empty treasures
From race to race, from one blood to another,
Beyond resistance of all human wisdom.

Therefore one people triumphs, and another
Languishes, in pursuance of her judgment,
Which hidden is, as in the grass a serpent.

Your knowledge has no counterstand against her;
She makes provision, judges, and pursues
Her governance, as theirs the other gods.

Her permutations have not any truce;
Necessity makes her precipitate,
So often cometh who his turn obtains.

And this is she who is so crucified
Even by those who ought to give her praise,
Giving her blame amiss, and bad repute.

But she is blissful, and she hears it not;
Among the other primal creatures gladsome
She turns her sphere, and blissful she rejoices.

Let us descend now unto greater woe;
Already sinks each star that was ascending
When I set out, and loitering is forbidden."

We crossed the circle to the other bank,

For all the gold beneath the moon,
Or ever has been, these weary souls
Could never make a single one last."

"Master," I said to him, "now tell me
What is this Fortune which you speak of
That has the world's goods in its clutches?"
He said: "Oh stupid creatures,
What kind of ignorance infects you?
Now I will tell you what I think of her.

He whose omniscience transcends all others
And created the heavens and gave a guide
So that every part is equal,

In the distribution of light;
Also gave a general mistress or guide
To do the same in mundane affairs

So she might change the fate
Of humanity, race to race and blood to blood,
At her will which is beyond human understanding.

Therefore, one people triumphs, while another
Languishes, in pursuit of her favor,
Which is hidden like a serpent in the grass.

Your knowledge of her has no effect;
She makes judgments, and governs
Like other gods.

Her modifications do not follow rules;
She works out of necessity,
When the time comes.

She is often criticized
Even by those who should praise her,
Blaming her for anything bad or amiss.

She is blissful, though, and does not hear it;
She focuses on other happy primal creatures
And blissfully rejoices.

Let us go deeper now to greater woe;
Already ascending stars are sinking
And loitering here is forbidden."

We crossed the circle to the other bank,

Near to a fount that boils, and pours itself
Along a gully that runs out of it.

The water was more sombre far than perse;
And we, in company with the dusky waves,
Made entrance downward by a path uncouth.

A marsh it makes, which has the name of Styx,
This tristful brooklet, when it has descended
Down to the foot of the malign gray shores.
And I, who stood intent upon beholding,
Saw people mud-besprent in that lagoon,
All of them naked and with angry look.

They smote each other not alone with hands,
But with the head and with the breast and feet,
Tearing each other piecemeal with their teeth.

Said the good Master: "Son, thou now beholdest
The souls of those whom anger overcame;
And likewise I would have thee know for certain

Beneath the water people are who sigh
And make this water bubble at the surface,
As the eye tells thee wheresoe'er it turns.

Fixed in the mire they say, 'We sullen were
In the sweet air, which by the sun is gladdened,
Bearing within ourselves the sluggish reek;

Now we are sullen in this sable mire.'
This hymn do they keep gurgling in their throats,
For with unbroken words they cannot say it."

Thus we went circling round the filthy fen
A great arc 'twixt the dry bank and the swamp,

With eyes turned unto those who gorge the mire;
Unto the foot of a tower we came at last.

Close to a boiling fountain pouring over itself
Along a gully that ran out of it.

The water was more somber;
And we, in the company of dusky waves,
Entered downward by way of an unworn path.

A marsh named Styx,
Created by the descending brook
Was down at the foot of the dark gray shores.
I stood intent on looking,
And saw people standing in mud
Naked and angry.

They hit each other not only with their hands,
But with their heads, breasts, and feet,
And tore each other apart with their teeth.

The good Master said: "Son, behold
The souls who were overcome by anger;
And I would like for you to know

People sigh beneath the water
Making the surface bubble,
As you see wherever you look.

They are stuck in the mire saying, 'We were sad
In the sweet air, which was gladdened by the sun,
Bearing within ourselves melancholia;

Now we are sullen in this black mire.'
They keep gurgling this mantra in their throats,
With unbroken words keeping them from speech."

Then we went around the circle of filth
Over a great arc between the dry bank and the
swamp,
Looking at those who stood steeped in the mire;
Until we came at last to the foot of a tower.

Inferno: Canto VIII

I say, continuing, that long before
We to the foot of that high tower had come,
Our eyes went upward to the summit of it,

By reason of two flamelets we saw placed there,
And from afar another answer them,
So far, that hardly could the eye attain it.

And, to the sea of all discernment turned,
I said: "What sayeth this, and what respondeth

That other fire? and who are they that made it?"

And he to me: "Across the turbid waves
What is expected thou canst now discern,
If reek of the morass conceal it not."

Cord never shot an arrow from itself
That sped away athwart the air so swift,
As I beheld a very little boat

Come o'er the water tow'rds us at that moment,
Under the guidance of a single pilot,
Who shouted, "Now art thou arrived, fell soul?"

"Phlegyas, Phlegyas, thou criest out in vain
For this once," said my Lord; "thou shalt not have us
Longer than in the passing of the slough."

As he who listens to some great deceit
That has been done to him, and then resents it,
Such became Phlegyas, in his gathered wrath.

My Guide descended down into the boat,
And then he made me enter after him,
And only when I entered seemed it laden.

Soon as the Guide and I were in the boat,
The antique prow goes on its way, dividing
More of the water than 'tis wont with others.

Continuing as we were before,
We came to the foot of a high tower,
Following with our eyes to its summit

Lit by two fires we saw placed there,
And two more at a distance
So far, we could hardly see them.

Trying to understand,
I said: "What does it mean, the two opposing pair
of fires
And who made them?"

He replied: "Across the cloudy waves
You cannot understand
If the marsh does hides it."

An arrow has never been shot
Through the air as swiftly,
As I saw a very little boat

Coming over the water towards us at that moment,
Under the guidance of a single pilot,
Who shouted, "Now you have arrived, fallen
soul?"
"Phlegyas, you are crying out in vain,"
Said my Lord; "You will not have us
Any longer than it takes to pass through this
slough."
Like one who listens to some great deceit
Done to him, and then resents it,
Phleguas filled with wrath.

My Guide descended down into the boat
And then made me enter after him
Making the boat seem heavy-laden.

As soon as we were in the boat,
The antique prow began to move,
Dividing the water more than necessary.

While we were running through the dead canal,	While we were transported through the dead canal,
Uprose in front of me one full of mire, And said, "Who 'rt thou that comest ere the hour?"	A being mired in the marsh rose up, And said, "Who are you coming here at this hour?"
And I to him: "Although I come, I stay not;	I said: "Although I come, I cannot stay;
But who art thou that hast become so squalid?" "Thou seest that I am one who weeps," he answered. And I to him: "With weeping and with wailing,	But, who are you who has become so wretched?" "You see I am the one who weeps," he answered. I said: "Please stay, poor spirit, with your weeping and wailing
Thou spirit maledict, do thou remain; For thee I know, though thou art all defiled."	For I think I know you, Although you are defiled."
Then stretched he both his hands unto the boat; Whereat my wary Master thrust him back, Saying, "Away there with the other dogs!"	Then he stretched both his hands into the boat; Where upon my wary Master threw him back, Saying, "Away with the other dogs!"
Thereafter with his arms he clasped my neck; He kissed my face, and said: "Disdainful soul, Blessed be she who bore thee in her bosom.	Then he clasped my neck with his arms; He kissed my face, and said: "Disdainful soul, Blessed be she who bore thee in her bosom.
That was an arrogant person in the world; Goodness is none, that decks his memory; So likewise here his shade is furious.	The most arrogant person in the world; No good lies in his memory, So, here he still is furious.
How many are esteemed great kings up there, Who here shall be like unto swine in mire, Leaving behind them horrible dispraises!"	How many esteemed great kings up there, Will be like pigs in mire, Leaving behind horrible words of praise!"
And I: "My Master, much should I be pleased, If I could see him soused into this broth, Before we issue forth out of the lake."	I said: "My Master, I would be pleased, If I could see him drowned into this water, Before we leave this lake."
And he to me: "Ere unto thee the shore Reveal itself, thou shalt be satisfied; Such a desire 'tis meet thou shouldst enjoy."	He replied: "Look there is the shore, Where you will be satisfied; By your desire."
A little after that, I saw such havoc Made of him by the people of the mire, That still I praise and thank my God for it.	A little after that, I saw such a havoc fall upon him Made by the people of the mire, I thanked God for it.
They all were shouting, "At Philippo Argenti!" And that exasperate spirit Florentine Turned round upon himself with his own teeth.	They were all shouting, "At Philippo Argenti!" And that exasperated spirit, Florentine Turned on himself with his own teeth.
We left him there, and more of him I tell not;	We left him there, and I will not speak anymore of him;

But on mine ears there smote a lamentation, Whence forward I intent unbar mine eyes.	*But I heard such a sorrowful lamentation,* *I could not look.*
And the good Master said: "Even now, my Son, The city draweth near whose name is Dis, With the grave citizens, with the great throng."	*The good Master said: "Now, my Son,* *The city whose name is Dis, draws near,* *With a great throng of grave citizens."*
And I: "Its mosques already, Master, clearly Within there in the valley I discern Vermilion, as if issuing from the fire	*I replied: "I see the mosques already, Master* *Where I think I see the valley* *Vermilion, as if issuing from the fire."*
They were." And he to me: "The fire eternal That kindles them within makes them look red, As thou beholdest in this nether Hell."	*He returned: "The eternal fire* *That burns them within makes them look red,* *As you can see in this Hell."*
Then we arrived within the moats profound, That circumvallate that disconsolate city; The walls appeared to me to be of iron.	*Then we arrived within the profound moats* *That circled the disconsolate city;* *The walls appeared to be of iron.*
Not without making first a circuit wide, We came unto a place where loud the pilot Cried out to us, "Debark, here is the entrance."	*Making a wide circuit,* *We came to a place where the pilot loudly cried,* *"Debark, here. This is the entrance."*
More than a thousand at the gates I saw Out of the Heavens rained down, who angrily Were saying, "Who is this that without death	*I saw more than a thousand at the gates* *Raining down as if from Heaven and who said angrily,* *"Who is this that without death*
Goes through the kingdom of the people dead?" And my sagacious Master made a sign Of wishing secretly to speak with them.	*Goes through the kingdom of the dead people?"* *My sagacious Master made a sign* *To speak secretly with them.*
A little then they quelled their great disdain, And said: "Come thou alone, and he begone Who has so boldly entered these dominions.	*They put away their disdain,* *And said: "You come alone, and send him* *Who has so boldly entered these dominions.*
Let him return alone by his mad road; Try, if he can; for thou shalt here remain, Who hast escorted him through such dark regions."	*Let him return alone by his mad road;* *If he can try; For you shall stay here* *Who has escorted him through such dark* *regions."*
Think, Reader, if I was discomforted At utterance of the accursed words; For never to return here I believed.	*Reader, think if I was discomforted by the* *Utterance of the accursed words;* *I believed I would never return from here.*
"O my dear Guide, who more than seven times Hast rendered me security, and drawn me From imminent peril that before me stood,	*"Oh my dear Guide, who has rendered me securely* *Seven times and saved me* *From imminent peril,*

Do not desert me," said I, "thus undone;
And if the going farther be denied us,
Let us retrace our steps together swiftly."

And that Lord, who had led me thitherward,
Said unto me: "Fear not; because our passage
None can take from us, it by Such is given.
But here await me, and thy weary spirit
Comfort and nourish with a better hope;
For in this nether world I will not leave thee."

So onward goes and there abandons me
My Father sweet, and I remain in doubt,
For No and Yes within my head contend.

I could not hear what he proposed to them;
But with them there he did not linger long,
Ere each within in rivalry ran back.

They closed the portals, those our adversaries,
On my Lord's breast, who had remained without
And turned to me with footsteps far between.

His eyes cast down, his forehead shorn had he
Of all its boldness, and he said, with sighs,
"Who has denied to me the dolesome houses?"

And unto me: "Thou, because I am angry,
Fear not, for I will conquer in the trial,
Whatever for defence within be planned.

This arrogance of theirs is nothing new;
For once they used it at less secret gate,
Which finds itself without a fastening still.

O'er it didst thou behold the dead inscription;
And now this side of it descends the steep,
Passing across the circles without escort,

One by whose means the city shall be opened."

Do not desert me," I said,
And if we are denied to go any farther,
Let us retrace our steps together swiftly."

The Lord, who led me here,
Said to me: "Fear not; because our passage
Cannot be taken from us.
But wait here for me, comfort and nourish
Your weary spirit with hope,
Because I will not leave you in this nether world."

So onward he went abandoning me,
My sweet Father, and I remained in doubt
Restless with discontent.

I could not near what he proposed to them;
But he did not linger long,
For each within ran back in rivalry.

Our adversaries closed the doors,
On my Lord's breast, who remained outside
And returned to me with long strides.

With his eyes cast down, and his face absent
Of its previous boldness, he said,
"Who has denied me access to the houses of
suffering?
Do not fear, because I am angry,
For I will conquer this battle
No matter what defense I must plan.

This arrogance of theirs is nothing new;
For once they used it at a less secret gate,
Which still has no fastening.

It bore the inscription of the dead;
Now it descends on this side of the bank,
Passing across the circles without escort,

Opening the city."

Inferno: Canto IX

That hue which cowardice brought out on me,
Beholding my Conductor backward turn,
Sooner repressed within him his new colour.

He stopped attentive, like a man who listens,
Because the eye could not conduct him far
Through the black air, and through the heavy fog.

"Still it behoveth us to win the fight,"
Began he; "Else. . .Such offered us herself. . .
O how I long that some one here arrive!"

Well I perceived, as soon as the beginning
He covered up with what came afterward,
That they were words quite different from the first;

But none the less his saying gave me fear,
Because I carried out the broken phrase,
Perhaps to a worse meaning than he had.

"Into this bottom of the doleful conch
Doth any e'er descend from the first grade,
Which for its pain has only hope cut off?"

This question put I; and he answered me:
"Seldom it comes to pass that one of us
Maketh the journey upon which I go.

True is it, once before I here below
Was conjured by that pitiless Erictho,
Who summoned back the shades unto their bodies.

Naked of me short while the flesh had been,
Before within that wall she made me enter
To bring a spirit from the circle of Judas;

That is the lowest region and the darkest,
And farthest from the heaven which circles all.
Well know I the way; therefore be reassured.

This fen, which a prodigious stench exhales,

The color of cowardice on my face,
As I beheld my Conductor turned backwards,
Was soon repressed by his new color.

He stopped and listened attentively,
Because he could not see very far
Through the black air and heavy fog.

"It still behooves us to win the fight,"
He began; "Else... offered us herself...
Oh, how I want someone to come!"

As soon as I perceived his statement,
He covered it up with
Words, quite different in nature;

But nevertheless his words scared me,
Because I took the meaning of his words
Perhaps worse than he intended.

"Into the bottom of this sad shell,
No one descends from the first circle,
Which only hope cuts off its pain?

I asked, and he answered:
"It seldom comes to pass that one of us
Makes the journey we are on.

It is true, I once came here before
Conjured by that pitiless Erictho,
Who called the spirits back to their bodies.

While I was still flesh,
And before I entered that wall, she made me enter
To bring a spirit from the circle of Judas;

That is the lowest and darkest region,
And the farthest from the heaven which circles all.
Therefore, be reassured, I know the way.

This marsh which exhales an extraordinary
stench,

Encompasses about the city dolent,
Where now we cannot enter without anger."

And more he said, but not in mind I have it;
Because mine eye had altogether drawn me
Tow'rds the high tower with the red-flaming summit,

Where in a moment saw I swift uprisen
The three infernal Furies stained with blood,
Who had the limbs of women and their mien,

And with the greenest hydras were begirt;
Small serpents and cerastes were their tresses,
Wherewith their horrid temples were entwined.

And he who well the handmaids of the Queen
Of everlasting lamentation knew,
Said unto me: "Behold the fierce Erinnys.

This is Megaera, on the left-hand side;
She who is weeping on the right, Alecto;
Tisiphone is between;" and then was silent.

Each one her breast was rending with her nails;
They beat them with their palms, and cried so loud,

That I for dread pressed close unto the Poet.

"Medusa come, so we to stone will change him!"
All shouted looking down; "in evil hour
Avenged we not on Theseus his assault!"

"Turn thyself round, and keep thine eyes close shut,
For if the Gorgon appear, and thou shouldst see it,
No more returning upward would there be."

Thus said the Master; and he turned me round
Himself, and trusted not unto my hands
So far as not to blind me with his own.

O ye who have undistempered intellects,
Observe the doctrine that conceals itself
Beneath the veil of the mysterious verses!

And now there came across the turbid waves
The clangour of a sound with terror fraught,
Because of which both of the margins trembled;
Not otherwise it was than of a wind

Encompasses the dolente city,
Where we cannot enter without anger."

He said more, but I don't remember it;
Because I was preoccupied with the
High tower with the flaming red summit,

Where I saw
The three infernal Furies, stained with blood,
Who were half women

And half serpent;
Small snakes and vipers made up their hair
Intertwining their heads.

And he who knew the handmaids of the Queen
Of everlasting lamentation,
Said: "Behold the fierce Erinnys.

This is Magaera, on the left;
The one weeping on the right is Alecto;
Tisiphone is between;" Then he was silent.

Each one was tearing at her breasts;
They beat them with their palms and cried so
loudly
I pressed closer to the Poet with dread.

"Medusa come, so we can change him to stone!"
They shouted looking down; " Upon this evil hour
Avenge us for the assault of Theseus!"

"Turn yourself around and keep your eyes closed,
For if the Gorgon appears and you should see,
You would not be able to return from here."

The Master said to me and he turned me around
Himself, and trusting not my hands
He covered my eyes with his own.

Oh you who have diseased intellect,
Observe the doctrine that conceals itself
Beneath the veil of the mysterious verses!

Then coming across the murky waves
I heard a terrifying sound,
Causing the sides of the marsh to tremble;
It was like the wind

Impetuous on account of adverse heats,
That smites the forest, and, without restraint,

The branches rends, beats down, and bears away;

Right onward, laden with dust, it goes superb,
And puts to flight the wild beasts and the shepherds.

Mine eyes he loosed, and said: "Direct the nerve
Of vision now along that ancient foam,
There yonder where that smoke is most intense."

Even as the frogs before the hostile serpent
Across the water scatter all abroad,
Until each one is huddled in the earth.

More than a thousand ruined souls I saw,
Thus fleeing from before one who on foot
Was passing o'er the Styx with soles unwet.

From off his face he fanned that unctuous air,
Waving his left hand oft in front of him,
And only with that anguish seemed he weary.

Well I perceived one sent from Heaven was he,
And to the Master turned; and he made sign
That I should quiet stand, and bow before him.

Ah! how disdainful he appeared to me!
He reached the gate, and with a little rod
He opened it, for there was no resistance.

"O banished out of Heaven, people despised!"
Thus he began upon the horrid threshold;
"Whence is this arrogance within you couched?

Wherefore recalcitrate against that will,
From which the end can never be cut off,
And which has many times increased your pain?

What helpeth it to butt against the fates?
Your Cerberus, if you remember well,
For that still bears his chin and gullet peeled."

Then he returned along the miry road,
And spake no word to us, but had the look
Of one whom other care constrains and goads

Caused by aversive heat,
Smiting the forest without restraint,

Beating down the branches and tearing them
away;
Going onward, laden with dust
Scattering the wild beasts and shepherds.

He uncovered my eyes and said: "Look
At the waves,
Where the smoke is most intense."

Like frogs who run before the hostile serpent
Across the water,
Until each one is huddled on the earth,

I saw more than a thousand ruined souls,
Fleeing from one who was
Passing over the river Styx by foot who remained
dry.
He fanned the unctuous air from his face,
Waving his left hand in front of him,
Making him seem weary.

I perceived he to be from Heaven,
So, I turned to the master,
Who made a sign I should be quiet and bow before
him.
He appeared disdainful
As he reached the gate and with a little rod
Opened it without resistance.

"Oh banished people despised by Heaven!"
He began upon the horrid threshold;
"Where do you get this arrogance?

Rejecting the will,
From which the end is eternal,
And that has increased your pain many times?

What does it help to butt against the fates?
Don't you remember your Cerberus,
Who still bears a peeled chin and gullet for that?"

Then he returned along the miry road,
And spoke no more to us, but had the look
Of one goaded by other cares

Than that of him who in his presence is; And we our feet directed tow'rds the city, After those holy words all confident.	Than those in his presence; We directed our feet towards the city, Filled with confidence after these holy words.
Within we entered without any contest; And I, who inclination had to see What the condition such a fortress holds,	So, we entered without contest; And I, inclined to see The condition the fortress held
Soon as I was within, cast round mine eye, And see on every hand an ample plain, Full of distress and torment terrible.	Looked around when inside And saw an ample plain, Full of distress and terrible torment.
Even as at Arles, where stagnant grows the Rhone, Even as at Pola near to the Quarnaro, That shuts in Italy and bathes its borders,	Like at Arles, where the Rhone grows stagnant, And at Pola near the Quarnaro, That shuts in Italy bathing its borders,
The sepulchres make all the place uneven; So likewise did they there on every side, Saving that there the manner was more bitter;	Making the place uneven, I saw a similar scene on every side But with much more bitterness,
For flames between the sepulchres were scattered,	For the flames between the sepulchers were scattered,
By which they so intensely heated were, That iron more so asks not any art.	By which they were so intensely heated, That they could burn iron.
All of their coverings uplifted were, And from them issued forth such dire laments, Sooth seemed they of the wretched and tormented.	All of their coverings were uplifted, And they issued forth dire laments that They made the wretched and tormented seem calm.
And I: "My Master, what are all those people Who, having sepulture within those tombs, Make themselves audible by doleful sighs?"	I asked: "My Master, what are all those people Enclosed in those tombs, Making themselves audible with their sad sighs?"
And he to me: "Here are the Heresiarchs, With their disciples of all sects, and much More than thou thinkest laden are the tombs.	He replied: "Her are the Heretics, With their disciples from all sects, And much more than you think are in the tombs.
Here like together with its like is buried; And more and less the monuments are heated." And when he to the right had turned, we passed	Together they are buried here; Their monuments are hated." He turned to the right and we passed
Between the torments and high parapets.	Between the tormented and the high parapets.

Inferno: Canto X

Now onward goes, along a narrow path Between the torments and the city wall, My Master, and I follow at his back.	*We went onward along a narrow path Between the tormented and the city wall, I following the Master.*
"O power supreme, that through these impious circles	*"Oh supreme power, that turns me through these impious circles,"*
Turnest me," I began, "as pleases thee, Speak to me, and my longings satisfy;	*I began, "If you will, Speak to me and tell me what I want to know;*
The people who are lying in these tombs, Might they be seen? already are uplifted The covers all, and no one keepeth guard."	*The people lying in these tombs, Might they be seen? Their covers are all uplifted and no one keeps guard."*
And he to me: "They all will be closed up When from Jehoshaphat they shall return Here with the bodies they have left above.	*He says to me, "They will all be closed When from the king of Judah they shall come back With the bodies they have left in heaven*
Their cemetery have upon this side With Epicurus all his followers, Who with the body mortal make the soul;	*"Their cemetery upon this side is With Epicurus and all his followers, Who makes the soul of the mortal body;*
But in the question thou dost put to me, Within here shalt thou soon be satisfied, And likewise in the wish thou keepest silent."	*So as for your question, You will soon have your answer, But you must keep quiet."*
And I: "Good Leader, I but keep concealed From thee my heart, that I may speak the less, Nor only now hast thou thereto disposed me."	*I said: "Good Leader, I keep my heart Concealed to speak less, Only to have you dispose me now."*
"O Tuscan, thou who through the city of fire Goest alive, thus speaking modestly, Be pleased to stay thy footsteps in this place.	*"Oh Tuscan, you who go through the city of fire Alive, speak modestly, And watch your step in this place.*
Thy mode of speaking makes thee manifest A native of that noble fatherland, To which perhaps I too molestful was."	*Your manner of speaking Reveals you are native to that noble fatherland, Where perhaps I was too molestful."*
Upon a sudden issued forth this sound From out one of the tombs; wherefore I pressed, Fearing, a little nearer to my Leader.	*All of sudden a sound issued forth From one of the tombs, so I pressed Fearfully closer to my leader.*
And unto me he said: "Turn thee; what dost thou?	*He said to me: "What are you doing?*

Behold there Farinata who has risen;
From the waist upwards wholly shalt thou see him."

There is Farinata who has risen;
You may see him from the waist up."

I had already fixed mine eyes on his,
And he uprose erect with breast and front
E'en as if Hell he had in great despite.

I had already fixed my eyes upon his,
As he arose exposing his front
Despite his great Hell.

And with courageous hands and prompt my Leader
Thrust me between the sepulchres towards him.
Exclaiming, "Let thy words explicit be."

Prompted by my Leader, with courageous hands
I thrust myself between the graves towards him,
Exclaiming, "Let your words be explicit."

As soon as I was at the foot of his tomb
Somewhat he eyed me, and, as if disdainful,
Then asked of me, "Who were thine ancestors?"

As soon as I was at the foot of his tomb
He eyed me disdainfully,
Then asked, "Who are your ancestors?"

I, who desirous of obeying was,
Concealed it not, but all revealed to him;
Whereat he raised his brows a little upward.

I, desiring to be obedient,
Told him everything,
Whereupon he raised his eyebrows upward.

Then said he: "Fiercely adverse have they been
To me, and to my fathers, and my party;
So that two several times I scattered them."

Then he said: "They have been fierce adversaries
To me, my fathers and my party;
So that I scattered them several times."

"If they were banished, they returned on all sides,"

"If they were banished, they returned more
ready,"

I answered him, "the first time and the second;
But yours have not acquired that art aright."

I answered him, "the first time and the second;
But yours have not acquired that art, yet."

Then there uprose upon the sight, uncovered
Down to the chin, a shadow at his side;
I think that he had risen on his knees.

Then, another arose uncovered
Down to the chin, like a shadow at his side;
I thought he had risen to his knees.

Round me he gazed, as if solicitude
He had to see if some one else were with me,
But after his suspicion was all spent,

He gazed around me
As if to see if I were alone,
But after his suspicion was extinguished,

Weeping, he said to me: "If through this blind

He said tearfully: "If you go through this blind
prison

Prison thou goest by loftiness of genius,
Where is my son? and why is he not with thee?"

By the loftiness of genius,
Where is my son and why is he not with you?"

And I to him: "I come not of myself;
He who is waiting yonder leads me here,
Whom in disdain perhaps your Guido had."

I replied: "I do not come of my own accord;
The one waiting over there is leading me,
Whom your Guido holds disdainfully."

His language and the mode of punishment
Already unto me had read his name;
On that account my answer was so full.

His language and mode of punishment
Had revealed his name to me;
So, I gave him my best answer.

Up starting suddenly, he cried out: "How
Saidst thou,--he had? Is he not still alive?
Does not the sweet light strike upon his eyes?"

When he became aware of some delay,
Which I before my answer made, supine
He fell again, and forth appeared no more.

But the other, magnanimous, at whose desire
I had remained, did not his aspect change,
Neither his neck he moved, nor bent his side.

"And if," continuing his first discourse,
"They have that art," he said, "not learned aright,
That more tormenteth me, than doth this bed.

But fifty times shall not rekindled be
The countenance of the Lady who reigns here,
Ere thou shalt know how heavy is that art;

And as thou wouldst to the sweet world return,
Say why that people is so pitiless
Against my race in each one of its laws?"

Whence I to him: "The slaughter and great carnage
Which have with crimson stained the Arbia, cause
Such orisons in our temple to be made."

After his head he with a sigh had shaken,
"There I was not alone," he said, "nor surely
Without a cause had with the others moved.

But there I was alone, where every one
Consented to the laying waste of Florence,
He who defended her with open face."

"Ah! so hereafter may your seed repose,"
I him entreated, "solve for me that knot,
Which has entangled my conceptions here.

It seems that you can see, if I hear rightly,
Beforehand whatsoe'er time brings with it,
And in the present have another mode."

"We see, like those who have imperfect sight,
The things," he said, "that distant are from us;
So much still shines on us the Sovereign Ruler.

He cried out suddenly: "How
Do you say that he is not still alive?
Does the sweet light of day not shine upon him?"

When he denoted a delay
In my answer
He fell again and appeared no more.

But the other soul at whose desire
I had remained, did not detect any changes,
And did not move a muscle.

"And if," continuing our previous conversation,
"They have not learned that art,
I am more tormented.

But no matter what I do
The countenance of the Lady who reigns here,
You should know is heavier than that art;

Before you return to the sweet world,
Tell me why that people is so pitiless
In its laws against my race?"

I said to him: "The slaughter and great carnage
Which have stained the Arabia crimson,
Cause derision among our temple."

He shook his head with a sigh and said:
"I was not alone there
Nor without a cause.

But I was alone when everyone
Consented to destroying Florence,
And anyone who defended her openly."

"Ah! So here your soul lies in repose,"
I entreated, "Solve that knot for me
Which has entangled my conceptions here.

It seems that you can see, if I hear you right,
The future and what it holds,
But you cannot see the present."

"We see, like those with imperfect vision,
The things," he said, "that are distant from us;
As part of our punishment by the Sovereign Ruler.

When they draw near, or are, is wholly vain
Our intellect, and if none brings it to us,
Not anything know we of your human state.

Hence thou canst understand, that wholly dead

Will be our knowledge from the moment when
The portal of the future shall be closed."

Then I, as if compunctious for my fault,
Said: "Now, then, you will tell that fallen one,
That still his son is with the living joined.

And if just now, in answering, I was dumb,
Tell him I did it because I was thinking
Already of the error you have solved me."

And now my Master was recalling me,
Wherefore more eagerly I prayed the spirit
That he would tell me who was with him there.

He said: "With more than a thousand here I lie;
Within here is the second Frederick,
And the Cardinal, and of the rest I speak not."

Thereon he hid himself; and I towards
The ancient poet turned my steps, reflecting
Upon that saying, which seemed hostile to me.

He moved along; and afterward thus going,
He said to me, "Why art thou so bewildered?"
And I in his inquiry satisfied him.

"Let memory preserve what thou hast heard
Against thyself," that Sage commanded me,

"And now attend here;" and he raised his finger.

"When thou shalt be before the radiance sweet
Of her whose beauteous eyes all things behold,
From her thou'lt know the journey of thy life."

Unto the left hand then he turned his feet;
We left the wall, and went towards the middle,
Along a path that strikes into a valley,

Which even up there unpleasant made its stench.

When they draw nearer, the vanity
Of our intellect keeps us
From knowing the state of humanity.

Therefore you cannot understand, that we shall
not be completely dead
Until the knowledge of future
Is taken from us."

Then I said with great regret,
"Now, then you can tell that fallen one,
That his son is still alive.

And if I appeared dumb in answering earlier,
Tell him I did it because I was thinking
Of the error you had solved for me."

Then my master called for me,
Where I begged the spirit more eagerly
That he would tell me who was with him.

He said: "I lie here with more than a thousand;
The second Frederick, and the Cardinal are here
But I must not speak of the rest."

Then he hid himself and I
Turned towards the ancient poet
Reflecting on the hostile words.

He moved along and said:
"Why are you so bewildered?"
And I answered him.

"Let memory preserve what you have heard
Against yourself," he commanded me, raising his
finger
"And now attend to our journey.

When you stand before the sweet radiance
Of her whose beautiful eyes sees all things,
You will know the meaning of your life."

Then he turned and walked to the left;
We went towards the middle,
Along a valley path,

With an unpleasant stench.

Inferno: Canto XI

Upon the margin of a lofty bank Which great rocks broken in a circle made, We came upon a still more cruel throng;	*Upon the margin of a lofty bank* *Where broken rocks made a circle* *We came upon a still crueler throng;*
And there, by reason of the horrible Excess of stench the deep abyss throws out,	*And there, by some horrible reason* *Was an excess of stench thrown out from the deep* *abyss,*
We drew ourselves aside behind the cover	*So strong that we had to step aside behind the* *cover*
Of a great tomb, whereon I saw a writing, Which said: "Pope Anastasius I hold, Whom out of the right way Photinus drew."	*Of a great tomb, where I saw a writing,* *Which said: "Pope Anastasius lies here,* *Drawn out of the right way by Photinus."*
"Slow it behoveth our descent to be, So that the sense be first a little used To the sad blast, and then we shall not heed it."	*"It will behoove us to descend slowly,* *So that we become used to the stench* *And not be thrown back by it."*
The Master thus; and unto him I said, "Some compensation find, that the time pass not Idly;" and he: "Thou seest I think of that.	*The Master said and I replied,* *"Let's not pass the time idly;"* *And he said: "I agree.*
My son, upon the inside of these rocks," Began he then to say, "are three small circles, From grade to grade, like those which thou art leaving.	*My son, inside these rocks,"* *He began to say, "are three small circles* *Gradually graded like the ones before.*
They all are full of spirits maledict; But that hereafter sight alone suffice thee, Hear how and wherefore they are in constraint.	*They are full of pitiful spirits;* *So let sight suffice thee,* *And hear how and why they are here.*
Of every malice that wins hate in Heaven, Injury is the end; and all such end Either by force or fraud afflicteth others.	*For every malice hated by Heaven,* *Violent injury is the end; and all end* *Either by force or fraud against others.*
But because fraud is man's peculiar vice, More it displeases God; and so stand lowest The fraudulent, and greater dole assails them. All the first circle of the Violent is;	*Since fraud is man's peculiar vice,* *It displeases God the most; and so the lowest* *Circle is accompanied by the greatest suffering.* *All the first circle of the violent;*
But since force may be used against three persons, In three rounds 'tis divided and constructed.	*Since force may be used against three persons,* *Is divided into three rounds.*
To God, to ourselves, and to our neighbour can we	*To God, to ourselves and to our neighbors, we can*

Use force; I say on them and on their things,
As thou shalt hear with reason manifest.

Use force; Upon them or their things,
As you will come to understand.

A death by violence, and painful wounds,

Those who commit violent death with painful
wounds

Are to our neighbour given; and in his substance
Ruin, and arson, and injurious levies;

To a neighbor or those who
Defame his name or commit arson;

Whence homicides, and he who smites unjustly,
Marauders, and freebooters, the first round
Tormenteth all in companies diverse.

Also murderers and those with unjust spite,
Marauders, and freeloaders are in the first circle
Tormented in diverse company.

Man may lay violent hands upon himself
And his own goods; and therefore in the second

Man may also lay violent hands upon himself
And his own possessions; and therefore, in the
second
Circle must constantly repent

Round must perforce without avail repent

Whoever of your world deprives himself,
Who games, and dissipates his property,
And weepeth there, where he should jocund be.

Along with anyone who deprives himself,
Who gambles or loses his property,
Making him pitiful where he should be joyful.

Violence can be done the Deity,
In heart denying and blaspheming Him,
And by disdaining Nature and her bounty.

Violence can be done to God
In denying Him or blaspheming,
Or by destroying Nature and her bounty.

And for this reason doth the smallest round
Seal with its signet Sodom and Cahors,
And who, disdaining God, speaks from the heart.

For this reason the smallest round is
Sealed with the signet of Sodom and Cahors,
Who spoke badly of God.

Fraud, wherewithal is every conscience stung,
A man may practise upon him who trusts,
And him who doth no confidence imburse.

Fraud, that stings every conscience,
A man may practice upon someone he trusts,
Or one for which he has no confidence.

This latter mode, it would appear, dissevers
Only the bond of love which Nature makes;
Wherefore within the second circle nestle

This latter mode, it appears severs
The bond of love made by Nature;
So nestled within the second circle are

Hypocrisy, flattery, and who deals in magic,
Falsification, theft, and simony,

Hypocrites, flatterers and ones who deal in magic,
Falsification, theft, or the making of money by
selling sacraments,
Panderers and barraters, and other filth

Panders, and barrators, and the like filth.

By the other mode, forgotten is that love
Which Nature makes, and what is after added,
From which there is a special faith engendered.

By the other mode, love is forgotten
Which is made by Nature, and afterwards
A special faith is added.

Hence in the smallest circle, where the point is
Of the Universe, upon which Dis is seated,

There is the smallest circle, where the point
Of the Universe, Dis, is located, where

Whoe'er betrays for ever is consumed."

And I: "My Master, clear enough proceeds

Thy reasoning, and full well distinguishes
This cavern and the people who possess it.

But tell me, those within the fat lagoon,
Whom the wind drives, and whom the rain doth beat,
And who encounter with such bitter tongues,

Wherefore are they inside of the red city
Not punished, if God has them in his wrath,
And if he has not, wherefore in such fashion?"

And unto me he said: "Why wanders so
Thine intellect from that which it is wont?
Or, sooth, thy mind where is it elsewhere looking?

Hast thou no recollection of those words
With which thine Ethics thoroughly discusses
The dispositions three, that Heaven abides not,--

Incontinence, and Malice, and insane
Bestiality? and how Incontinence
Less God offendeth, and less blame attracts?

If thou regardest this conclusion well,
And to thy mind recallest who they are
That up outside are undergoing penance,

Clearly wilt thou perceive why from these felons
They separated are, and why less wroth
Justice divine doth smite them with its hammer."

"O Sun, that healest all distempered vision
Thou dost content me so, when thou resolvest,
That doubting pleases me no less than knowing!

Once more a little backward turn thee," said I,
"There where thou sayest that usury offends
Goodness divine, and disengage the knot."

"Philosophy," he said, "to him who heeds it,
Noteth, not only in one place alone,
After what manner Nature takes her course

From Intellect Divine, and from its art;

Whoever betrays is consumed forever."

I said: "My Master, your reasoning is clear enough
And distinguishes full well
This cavern and the people who possess it.

But tell me, who are they within the fat lagoon,
Whom the wind drives and the rain beats,
And who encounter with such bitter tongues,

Inside the red city where they are not punished,
If God has them in his wrath,
And if not, why are they in that situation?"

He replied: "Why do you wander
About that to which you are not accustomed,
Or soothe your mind by looking elsewhere?

Do you not remember those words
Discussed thoroughly in Ethics
About the three dispositions that Heaven does not abide,
Incontinence, Malice, and insane
Bestiality? Incontinence offends God less
And attracts less blame.

If you remember this conclusion well,
And recall who they are
Undergoing penance outside,

You will clearly perceive why these felons
Are separated and receive less wrath
Because divine Justice smites them with its hammer.
Oh Sun, that heals all distempered vision,
You do make me content, when you shed light,
So doubting pleases me no less than knowing!"

Once more turn a little backward," I said,
"To what you said about usury offending
Divine Goodness and disengaging the knot."

"Philosophy," he said, "to him who listens,
Notes not only in one place alone,
Does Nature take her course

From Divine Intellect and from its art;

And if thy Physics carefully thou notest,
After not many pages shalt thou find,

That this your art as far as possible
Follows, as the disciple doth the master;
So that your art is, as it were, God's grandchild.

From these two, if thou bringest to thy mind
Genesis at the beginning, it behoves
Mankind to gain their life and to advance;

And since the usurer takes another way,
Nature herself and in her follower
Disdains he, for elsewhere he puts his hope.

But follow, now, as I would fain go on,
For quivering are the Fishes on the horizon,
And the Wain wholly over Caurus lies,

And far beyond there we descend the crag."

And if you remember Physics, note
You will not find

That your art does not follow
Like the disciple does its master;
So that your understanding is God's grandchild.

From these two, if you remember
Genesis at the beginning, it behooves
Man to gain life and to advance;

And since the usurer takes another way,
Nature herself and her follower
Disdains he who puts his hope elsewhere.

But follow, now, as I go on,
For the Fishes are quivering on the horizon,
And the Wain lies over Caurus

From where we must descend the crag."

Inferno: Canto XII

The place where to descend the bank we came

Was alpine, and from what was there, moreover,
Of such a kind that every eye would shun it.

Such as that ruin is which in the flank
Smote, on this side of Trent, the Adige,
Either by earthquake or by failing stay,

For from the mountain's top, from which it moved,
Unto the plain the cliff is shattered so,
Some path 'twould give to him who was above;

Even such was the descent of that ravine,
And on the border of the broken chasm
The infamy of Crete was stretched along,

Who was conceived in the fictitious cow;

And when he us beheld, he bit himself,
Even as one whom anger racks within.

My Sage towards him shouted: "Peradventure
Thou think'st that here may be the Duke of Athens,
Who in the world above brought death to thee?

Get thee gone, beast, for this one cometh not
Instructed by thy sister, but he comes
In order to behold your punishments."

As is that bull who breaks loose at the moment
In which he has received the mortal blow,
Who cannot walk, but staggers here and there,

The Minotaur beheld I do the like;
And he, the wary, cried: "Run to the passage;
While he wroth, 'tis well thou shouldst descend."

Thus down we took our way o'er that discharge
Of stones, which oftentimes did move themselves
Beneath my feet, from the unwonted burden.

We came to the place where we descended the bank
Alpine and made up of such
That every eye would shun it.

Like the ruin which is flanked
On this side of Trent, the Adige,
Caused either by earthquake or by falling

From the mountain's top,
Unto the plain, the cliff was shattered so
A path was created for those above;

The descent of that ravine,
On the border of the broken chasm,
Like the infamous Crete, which was stretched along
Was guarded by one conceived by the fictitious cow;
Who beheld us and bit himself,
Like one whom is racked by anger.

My Sage shouted towards him: "Peradventure
Do you think that here is the Duke of Athens,
Who killed you in the world above?

Get gone, beast, for this one comes
Not instructed by your sister, but to
Behold your punishments."

Like the bull who breaks loose
As he receives the mortal blow,
And cannot walk, but staggers here and there,

The Minotaur looked at me
And my master cried: "Run to the passage;
You should descend while he is angry."

Thus, we took our way down over that discharge
Of stones, which moved
Beneath my feet from the unwonted burden.

Thoughtful I went; and he said: "Thou art thinking

Perhaps upon this ruin, which is guarded
By that brute anger which just now I quenched.
Now will I have thee know, the other time
I here descended to the nether Hell,
This precipice had not yet fallen down.

But truly, if I well discern, a little
Before His coming who the mighty spoil
Bore off from Dis, in the supernal circle,

Upon all sides the deep and loathsome valley
Trembled so, that I thought the Universe
Was thrilled with love, by which there are who think

The world ofttimes converted into chaos;
And at that moment this primeval crag
Both here and elsewhere made such overthrow.

But fix thine eyes below; for draweth near
The river of blood, within which boiling is
Whoe'er by violence doth injure others."

O blind cupidity, O wrath insane,
That spurs us onward so in our short life,
And in the eternal then so badly steeps us!

I saw an ample moat bent like a bow,
As one which all the plain encompasses,
Conformable to what my Guide had said.

And between this and the embankment's foot
Centaurs in file were running, armed with arrows,
As in the world they used the chase to follow.

Beholding us descend, each one stood still,
And from the squadron three detached themselves,
With bows and arrows in advance selected;

And from afar one cried: "Unto what torment
Come ye, who down the hillside are descending?
Tell us from there; if not, I draw the bow."

My Master said: "Our answer will we make
To Chiron, near you there; in evil hour,
That will of thine was evermore so hasty."

I went along thoughtfully and he said: "You are thinking
Upon this ruin, which is guarded
By that angry brute I just disarmed.
I will have you know, the other time
I was here in this nether Hell,
This precipice had not yet fallen down.

But if I remember truly, a little
Before His coming who the mighty spoil
Bore off from Dis, in the supernal circle,

The sides of the deep and loathsome valley
Trembled so, that I thought the Universe
Was thrilled with love, by which there are those who think
The world was converted into such chaos;
So at that moment this primeval crag
Both here and elsewhere was overthrown.

But fix your eyes below; for drawing nearer is
The river of blood, where those who
Injure others are boiling."

Oh blind love, Oh Insane wrath,
That spurs us onward in our short life,
So that we are so badly steeped in eternity!

I saw an ample moat bent like a bow,
Like one which encompasses all the plain,
Just like my Guide had said.

And between this and the foot of the embankment,
Centaurs were running, armed with arrows,
As in the world they were chased.

Seeing us descend, each one stood still,
And from the squadron three detached themselves,
And advanced with bows and arrows raised;

From afar one cried: "Unto what torment
Do you come down the hillside?
Tell us from there or I will draw the bow."

My Master said: "We will answer
To Chiron, near you there; in evil hour,
Your will is so hasty."

Then touched he me, and said: "This one is Nessus,	*Then he touched me and said: "This one is Nessus,*
Who perished for the lovely Dejanira,	*Who perished for the lovely Dejanira,*
And for himself, himself did vengeance take.	*And took vengeance upon himself.*
And he in the midst, who at his breast is gazing,	*And in the middle who is gazing at his breast*
Is the great Chiron, who brought up Achilles;	*Is the great Chiron, who brought up Achilles;*
That other Pholus is, who was so wrathful.	*That other, Pholus, who is so wrathful.*
Thousands and thousands go about the moat	*Thousands and thousands go about the moat*
Shooting with shafts whatever soul emerges	*Shooting with arrows whatever soul emerges*
Out of the blood, more than his crime allots."	*Out of the blood, more than his crime allows."*
Near we approached unto those monsters fleet;	*We approached nearer to the fleet of monsters;*
Chiron an arrow took, and with the notch	*Chiron took an arrow and*
Backward upon his jaws he put his beard.	*Pulled backward along his jaw and beard.*
After he had uncovered his great mouth,	*After he uncovered his great mouth,*
He said to his companions: "Are you ware	*He said to his companions: "Are you aware*
That he behind moveth whate'er he touches?	*That the one behind moves whatever he touches?*
Thus are not wont to do the feet of dead men."	*Thus, he does not have the feet of dead men."*
And my good Guide, who now was at his breast,	*And my good Guide, who now was at his breast,*
Where the two natures are together joined,	*Where the two animals are joined together,*
Replied: "Indeed he lives, and thus alone	*Replied: "Indeed he lives, and so it behooves*
Me it behoves to show him the dark valley;	*Me to show him the dark valley;*
Necessity, and not delight, impels us.	*It is necessity and not delight that compels us.*
Some one withdrew from singing Halleluja,	*Someone withdrew from singing Hallelujah,*
Who unto me committed this new office;	*And committed me this new task;*
No thief is he, nor I a thievish spirit.	*He is no thief nor a thievish spirit.*
But by that virtue through which I am moving	*But by the virtue that moves me and*
My steps along this savage thoroughfare,	*My steps along this savage way,*
Give us some one of thine, to be with us,	*Give us someone of yours to be with us,*
And who may show us where to pass the ford,	*And who may show us where to pass the ford,*
And who may carry this one on his back;	*And who may carry this one on his back;*
For 'tis no spirit that can walk the air."	*For he is no spirit that can walk on air."*
Upon his right breast Chiron wheeled about,	*Chiron wheeled about upon his right breast,*
And said to Nessus: "Turn and do thou guide them,	*And said to Nessus: "Turn and guide them,*
And warn aside, if other band may meet you."	*And warn the other band, if you meet them."*
We with our faithful escort onward moved	*We moved onward with our faithful escort*
Along the brink of the vermilion boiling,	*Along the brink of the boiling vermilion*
Wherein the boiled were uttering loud laments.	*Wherein the boiled were lamenting loudly.*

People I saw within up to the eyebrows,
And the great Centaur said: "Tyrants are these,
Who dealt in bloodshed and in pillaging.

Here they lament their pitiless mischiefs; here
Is Alexander, and fierce Dionysius
Who upon Sicily brought dolorous years.
That forehead there which has the hair so black
Is Azzolin; and the other who is blond,
Obizzo is of Esti, who, in truth,

Up in the world was by his stepson slain."
Then turned I to the Poet; and he said,
"Now he be first to thee, and second I."

A little farther on the Centaur stopped
Above a folk, who far down as the throat

Seemed from that boiling stream to issue forth.

A shade he showed us on one side alone,
Saying: "He cleft asunder in God's bosom
The heart that still upon the Thames is honoured."

Then people saw I, who from out the river
Lifted their heads and also all the chest;
And many among these I recognised.

Thus ever more and more grew shallower
That blood, so that the feet alone it covered;
And there across the moat our passage was.

"Even as thou here upon this side beholdest
The boiling stream, that aye diminishes,"
The Centaur said, "I wish thee to believe

That on this other more and more declines
Its bed, until it reunites itself
Where it behoveth tyranny to groan.

Justice divine, upon this side, is goading
That Attila, who was a scourge on earth,
And Pyrrhus, and Sextus; and for ever milks

The tears which with the boiling it unseals
In Rinier da Corneto and Rinier Pazzo,
Who made upon the highways so much war."

I saw people within up to their eyebrows,
And the great Centaur said: "These are tyrants
Who dealt in bloodshed and in pillaging.

They lament their pitiless mischief;
Here is Alexander and fierce Dionysius
Who brought suffering upon Sicily.
That forehead over there with the black hair
Is Azzolin; and the other who is blond,
is Obizzo of Esti, who in truth,

Was slain by his stepson up in the world."
Then I turned to the Poet and he said,
"Now, he is the first and I am the second to you."

A little farther on the Centaur stopped
Above a group of folk, who were as far down as
the throat
Seeming to boil forth in the stream.

He showed us a shade alone on one side,
Saying: "He cleft asunder in God's bosom
The heart that is still honored upon the Thames."

Then I saw people who from the river
Lifted their heads and also their chests;
And I recognized many among these.

Thus the river growing ever more shallower
With blood, so that the feet alone were covered;
There we crossed the moat.

"Even as you behold from this side
The boiling stream, that diminishes,"
The Centaur said, " I want you to believe

That on this other side more declines its bed,
Until it reunites itself
Where it holds tyrants to groan.

Divine Justice, upon this side, goads
That Attila, who was a scourge on earth,
And Pyrrhus, and Sextus; who forever milk

The tears which are unsealed by the boiling
Are Rinier da Corneto and Rinier Pazzo,
Who made so much war upon the highways."

Then back he turned, and passed again the ford.   *Then he turned back and passed the ford again.*

Inferno: Canto XIII

Not yet had Nessus reached the other side,
When we had put ourselves within a wood,
That was not marked by any path whatever.

Not foliage green, but of a dusky colour,
Not branches smooth, but gnarled and intertangled,

Not apple-trees were there, but thorns with poison.

Such tangled thickets have not, nor so dense,
Those savage wild beasts, that in hatred hold
'Twixt Cecina and Corneto the tilled places.

There do the hideous Harpies make their nests,
Who chased the Trojans from the Strophades,
With sad announcement of impending doom;

Broad wings have they, and necks and faces human,
And feet with claws, and their great bellies fledged;
They make laments upon the wondrous trees.

And the good Master: "Ere thou enter farther,
Know that thou art within the second round,"
Thus he began to say, "and shalt be, till

Thou comest out upon the horrible sand;
Therefore look well around, and thou shalt see
Things that will credence give unto my speech."

I heard on all sides lamentations uttered,
And person none beheld I who might make them,
Whence, utterly bewildered, I stood still.

I think he thought that I perhaps might think
So many voices issued through those trunks
From people who concealed themselves from us;

Therefore the Master said: "If thou break off
Some little spray from any of these trees,
The thoughts thou hast will wholly be made vain."

Then stretched I forth my hand a little forward,

He had not yet reached the other side,
When we had put ourselves within a wood,
That was not marked by any path.

No green foliage, but a dusky color,
No smooth branches, but gnarled and tangled ones,
No apple trees were there, but poisonous thorns.

There were no tangled thickets so dense,
That holds the savage wild beasts
Between Cecina and Corneto.

The hideous harpies made their nests there,
Who chased the Trojans from the Strophades,
With sad announcements of impending doom;

They had broad wings and human faces and necks
And feet with claws, and great fledged bellies;
They made laments upon the wondrous trees.

The good Master: "Before you go farther,
Know that you are within the second round,"
Then he began to say, "And you will be until

You come out upon the horrible sand;
Therefore look around and you will see
Things that will give credence to my speech."

I heard lamentations uttered on all sides,
But I did not see anyone who might make them,
So on utter bewilderment, I stood still.

He thought that I was thinking
So many voices issued through those trunks came
From people who concealed themselves from us;

Therefore the Master said: "If you break off
Some little spray from any of these trees,
You will realize your thoughts are in vain."

Then I stretched forth my hand,

And plucked a branchlet off from a great thorn;
And the trunk cried, "Why dost thou mangle me?"

After it had become embrowned with blood,
It recommenced its cry: "Why dost thou rend me?
Hast thou no spirit of pity whatsoever?

Men once we were, and now are changed to trees;

Indeed, thy hand should be more pitiful,
Even if the souls of serpents we had been."

As out of a green brand, that is on fire
At one of the ends, and from the other drips
And hisses with the wind that is escaping;

So from that splinter issued forth together
Both words and blood; whereat I let the tip
Fall, and stood like a man who is afraid.

"Had he been able sooner to believe,"
My Sage made answer, "O thou wounded soul,
What only in my verses he has seen,

Not upon thee had he stretched forth his hand;
Whereas the thing incredible has caused me
To put him to an act which grieveth me.

But tell him who thou wast, so that by way
Of some amends thy fame he may refresh
Up in the world, to which he can return."

And the trunk said: "So thy sweet words allure me,

I cannot silent be; and you be vexed not,
That I a little to discourse am tempted.

I am the one who both keys had in keeping
Of Frederick's heart, and turned them to and fro
So softly in unlocking and in locking,

That from his secrets most men I withheld;
Fidelity I bore the glorious office
So great, I lost thereby my sleep and pulses.

The courtesan who never from the dwelling
Of Caesar turned aside her strumpet eyes,
Death universal and the vice of courts,

And plucked a branch from a great tree;
And the trunk cried, "Why do you mangle me?"

After it became brown with blood,
It recommenced its cry: "Why do you rend me?
Have you no pity whatsoever?

We were once men and now we are changed to trees;
Indeed, your hand should be more pitiful,
Even if we were souls of serpents."

As out of a green brand, that is on fire
At one of the ends, and from the other drips
And hisses with the escaping wind,

So was from that splinter issuing forth
Both words and blood; whereat I let the tip
Fall, and stood like a scared man.

"Had he been able to believe sooner,"
My Sage answered, "Oh wounded soul,
For he has only seen my words,

He would not have stretched forth his hand;
Which I made him do
And it grieves me so.

But tell him who you were, so that by way
Of some amends, he may refresh your fame
Up in the world, to which he can return."

And the trunk said: "Your sweet words allure me so,
I cannot be silent;
So I am tempted.

I am the one who had both keys
Of Frederick's heart, and turned them to and fro
So softly with locking and unlocking,

That I withheld his secrets from most men;
I bore the glorious office with fidelity
So great, I lost much sleep and my heart.

The courtesan who never turned her eyes
From the dwelling of Caesar,
Universal death and the vice of courts,

Inflamed against me all the other minds,
And they, inflamed, did so inflame Augustus,
That my glad honours turned to dismal mournings.

My spirit, in disdainful exultation,
Thinking by dying to escape disdain,
Made me unjust against myself, the just.

I, by the roots unwonted of this wood,
Do swear to you that never broke I faith
Unto my lord, who was so worthy of honour;

And to the world if one of you return,
Let him my memory comfort, which is lying
Still prostrate from the blow that envy dealt it."

Waited awhile, and then: "Since he is silent,"
The Poet said to me, "lose not the time,
But speak, and question him, if more may please thee."

Whence I to him: "Do thou again inquire
Concerning what thou thinks't will satisfy me;
For I cannot, such pity is in my heart."

Therefore he recommenced: "So may the man
Do for thee freely what thy speech implores,
Spirit incarcerate, again be pleased

To tell us in what way the soul is bound
Within these knots; and tell us, if thou canst,
If any from such members e'er is freed."

Then blew the trunk amain, and afterward
The wind was into such a voice converted:
"With brevity shall be replied to you.

When the exasperated soul abandons
The body whence it rent itself away,
Minos consigns it to the seventh abyss.

It falls into the forest, and no part
Is chosen for it; but where Fortune hurls it,
There like a grain of spelt it germinates.

It springs a sapling, and a forest tree;
The Harpies, feeding then upon its leaves,
Do pain create, and for the pain an outlet.

Inflamed all the other minds against me,
And they inflamed Augustus,
So my honor turned to sad mourning.

My spirit, in disdainful exultation,
Thought that by dying, it would escape disdain,
Making me commit unjust acts against myself.

I, by the roots of this unwonted wood,
Swear to you that I never broke faith
Unto my lord, who was so worthy of honor.

And if you return to the world,
Comfort my memory, which is still lying
Prostrate from the blow dealt by envy."

A minute passed and then: "Since he is silent,"
The Poet said, "Lose no time
And question him, if it pleases you."

So I said to him: "Do you mind inquiring again
Concerning what you think will satisfy me;
For I cannot, I am overwhelmed with such pity."

Therefore he continued: "So the man
May freely do for you what you asked,
Incarcerated spirit, please

Tell us in what way the soul is bound
Within these knots; and tell us, if you can
If any from here is ever freed."

Then the trunk blew and afterward
The wind converted into a voice saying:
"I shall reply to you with brevity.

When the exasperated soul abandons
The body by suicide,
Minos consigns it to the seventh abyss.

It falls into the forest, and no part
Is chosen for it; but where Fortune hurls it
It germinates like a grain of spelt.

It springs a sapling and a forest tree;
The Harpies, feeding upon its leaves,
Create pain and an outlet.

Like others for our spoils shall we return;
But not that any one may them revest,
For 'tis not just to have what one casts off.

Here we shall drag them, and along the dismal
Forest our bodies shall suspended be,
Each to the thorn of his molested shade."
We were attentive still unto the trunk,
Thinking that more it yet might wish to tell us,
When by a tumult we were overtaken,

In the same way as he is who perceives
The boar and chase approaching to his stand,
Who hears the crashing of the beasts and branches;

And two behold! upon our left-hand side,
Naked and scratched, fleeing so furiously,
That of the forest, every fan they broke.

He who was in advance: "Now help, Death, help!"
And the other one, who seemed to lag too much,
Was shouting: "Lano, were not so alert

Those legs of thine at joustings of the Toppo!"
And then, perchance because his breath was failing,
He grouped himself together with a bush.

Behind them was the forest full of black
She-mastiffs, ravenous, and swift of foot
As greyhounds, who are issuing from the chain.

On him who had crouched down they set their teeth,

And him they lacerated piece by piece,
Thereafter bore away those aching members.

Thereat my Escort took me by the hand,
And led me to the bush, that all in vain
Was weeping from its bloody lacerations.

"O Jacopo," it said, "of Sant' Andrea,
What helped it thee of me to make a screen?
What blame have I in thy nefarious life?"

When near him had the Master stayed his steps,
He said: "Who wast thou, that through wounds so many
Art blowing out with blood thy dolorous speech?"

Like others, we shall return for our spoils;
But not to reinvest in them
For one cannot have what it casts off.

Here we drag them along the dismal
Forest where our bodies are suspended
From the thorn of its molested shade."
We were still attentive to the trunk,
Thinking it might wish to tell us more,
When we were overtaken by a tumult.

In the same way as one who perceives
The chase of a boar approaching him,
And hears the crashing of beast and branches;

We saw two people upon our left-hand side,
Naked and scratched, they fled so furiously,
That they broke every limb of the forest.

The first: "Now help, Death, help!"
The other one, who seemed to lag too much,
Was shouting: "Lano, your legs were not so alert

At the jousting of the Toppo!"
And then, perhaps because of his failing breath,
He fell into a bush.

Behind them, the forest was full of black
Female mastiffs, ravenous and quick
As greyhounds, issuing from a chain.

They set their teeth on the one who had crouched down,
Lacerating him piece by piece,
And bearing away his members.

Then my Escort took me by the hand,
And led me to the bush, that in vain
Was weeping from its bloody lacerations.

"Oh Jacopo," it said, "of Saint Andrea,
What did it help for me to make a screen?
Why do you blame me in this nefarious life?"

When the Master drew nearer,
He said: "Who were you, speaking
Such pitiful words through so many wounds?"

And he to us: "O souls, that hither come
To look upon the shameful massacre
That has so rent away from me my leaves,

Gather them up beneath the dismal bush;
I of that city was which to the Baptist
Changed its first patron, wherefore he for this

Forever with his art will make it sad.
And were it not that on the pass of Arno
Some glimpses of him are remaining still,

Those citizens, who afterwards rebuilt it
Upon the ashes left by Attila,
In vain had caused their labour to be done.

Of my own house I made myself a gibbet.

And he said to us: "Oh souls that have come here
To look upon the shameful massacre
That has torn away my leaves,

Gather them up beneath the dismal bush;
I was of that city which to the Baptist
Changed its first patron, wherefore he

Forever changed with his art and made it sad.
And upon the pass of Arno
Some glimpses of him still remain

Due to those citizens, who rebuilt it
Upon the ashes left by Attila,
Causing their labor to be done in vain.

From my own house, I made myself a gallows."

Inferno: Canto XIV

Because the charity of my native place Constrained me, gathered I the scattered leaves, And gave them back to him, who now was hoarse.	*Because the charity of my native place* *Constrained me, I gathered the scattered leaves,* *And gave them back to him, who was now hoarse.*
Then came we to the confine, where disparted The second round is from the third, and where A horrible form of Justice is beheld.	*The we came to the confine, where* *The second round parted from the third,* *And where I saw a horrible form of Justice.*
Clearly to manifest these novel things, I say that we arrived upon a plain, Which from its bed rejecteth every plant;	*To manifest clearly these things,* *I say we arrived upon a plain,* *Which rejected from its bed every plant;*
The dolorous forest is a garland to it All round about, as the sad moat to that; There close upon the edge we stayed our feet.	*The sad forest is a garland to it* *All around like a sad moat* *So we stayed close upon the edge.*
The soil was of an arid and thick sand, Not of another fashion made than that Which by the feet of Cato once was pressed.	*The soil was a dry and thick sand,* *Like that made in the same fashion as* *That by the feet of Cato was pressed.*
Vengeance of God, O how much oughtest thou By each one to be dreaded, who doth read That which was manifest unto mine eyes!	*Vengeance of God, oh how much* *Each should dread, who read* *That which I saw with my own eyes!*
Of naked souls beheld I many herds, Who all were weeping very miserably, And over them seemed set a law diverse.	*I saw many naked souls* *Who were weeping very miserably,* *Over which a diverse law seemed set.*
Supine upon the ground some folk were lying; And some were sitting all drawn up together, And others went about continually.	*Some folk were lying supine upon the ground;* *And some were sitting all drawn up together,* *While others moved continually about.*
Those who were going round were far the more, And those were less who lay down to their torment, But had their tongues more loosed to lamentation.	*More were moving around than* *Those lying down, who* *Loosed their tongues with lamentation.*
O'er all the sand-waste, with a gradual fall, Were raining down dilated flakes of fire, As of the snow on Alp without a wind.	*Over all the sand, with a gradual flow* *Rain fell down like dilated flakes of fire,* *And snow on the windless Alps.*
As Alexander, in those torrid parts Of India, beheld upon his host	*As Alexander, in those torrid parts* *Of India inflicted upon his host,*

Flames fall unbroken till they reached the ground.

Whence he provided with his phalanxes
To trample down the soil, because the vapour
Better extinguished was while it was single;

Thus was descending the eternal heat,
Whereby the sand was set on fire, like tinder
Beneath the steel, for doubling of the dole.

Without repose forever was the dance
Of miserable hands, now there, now here,
Shaking away from off them the fresh gleeds.

"Master," began I, "thou who overcomest
All things except the demons dire, that issued
Against us at the entrance of the gate,

Who is that mighty one who seems to heed not
The fire, and lieth lowering and disdainful,
So that the rain seems not to ripen him?"

And he himself, who had become aware
That I was questioning my Guide about him,
Cried: "Such as I was living, am I, dead.

If Jove should weary out his smith, from whom
He seized in anger the sharp thunderbolt,
Wherewith upon the last day I was smitten,

And if he wearied out by turns the others
In Mongibello at the swarthy forge,
Vociferating, 'Help, good Vulcan, help!'

Even as he did there at the fight of Phlegra,
And shot his bolts at me with all his might,
He would not have thereby a joyous vengeance."

Then did my Leader speak with such great force,
That I had never heard him speak so loud:
"O Capaneus, in that is not extinguished

Thine arrogance, thou punished art the more;
Not any torment, saving thine own rage,
Would be unto thy fury pain complete."

Then he turned round to me with better lip,
Saying: "One of the Seven Kings was he

Flames fell unbroken until they reached the ground.
Where he ordered his army
To trample down the soil, because the vapor
Extinguished better while it was single;

Thus the descending and eternal heat set
The sand on fire, like tinder
Beneath the steel, for the doubling of suffering.

The dance was forever without repose
Of miserable hands, now here then there
Shaking away from them a glowing coal.

"Master," I began, "those who overcome
All things except the demons dire,
That was issued against us at the entrance of the gate,
Who is the mighty one who seems to not heed
The fire, and lies lower,
So that the rain seems not to touch him?"

And he, who had become aware
That I was questioning my Guide about him,
Cried: "I am dead the same way I was living.

If Jove should use his smith, from whom
He seized in anger the sharp thunderbolt,
With which I was killed,

And if he turned to others
In Mongibello at the swarthy forge,
Saying, 'Help, good Vulcan, help!'

Even as he did at the fight of Phlegra,
And shot his bolts at me with all his might,
He would not have a joyous vengeance."

Then my Leader spoke with such great force,
Like I had never heard him speak before:
"Oh Capaneus, since your arrogance is not extinguished
You are punished all the more;
No torment, except your own rage,
Would make your pain complete."

Then he turned around to me with better lip,
Saying: "He was one of the Seven Kings

Who Thebes besieged, and held, and seems to hold	Who besieged Thebes, and held, and seems to still hold
God in disdain, and little seems to prize him; But, as I said to him, his own despites Are for his breast the fittest ornaments.	God in disdain, and little seems to pain him; But, as I said to him, his own spitefulness Are the best ornaments for this breast.
Now follow me, and mind thou do not place As yet thy feet upon the burning sand, But always keep them close unto the wood."	Now follow me, and do not place Your feet upon the burning sand, Staying close to the wood instead."
Speaking no word, we came to where there gushes Forth from the wood a little rivulet, Whose redness makes my hair still stand on end.	Without a word, we came to where there gushes Forth from the wood a little river, Whose redness made my hair stand on end.
As from the Bulicame springs the brooklet,	The brook, appearing as if it sprang from the Bulicame,
The sinful women later share among them, So downward through the sand it went its way.	Shared by sinful women, Ran downward through the sand.
The bottom of it, and both sloping banks, Were made of stone, and the margins at the side;	The bottom of it and both sloping banks Were made of stone and upon the margins at the side
Whence I perceived that there the passage was.	I perceived a passage there.
"In all the rest which I have shown to thee Since we have entered in within the gate Whose threshold unto no one is denied,	"In all the rest which I have shown you Since we have entered within the gate Whose threshold no one is denied,
Nothing has been discovered by thine eyes So notable as is the present river, Which all the little flames above it quenches."	Nothing has been discovered by my eyes As notable as the river, Which quenched all the little flames above it."
These words were of my Leader; whence I prayed him	These words were my Leader's; Whereupon I asked him
That he would give me largess of the food, For which he had given me largess of desire.	If he would give me the gift of food To feed the gift he gave me of desire.
"In the mid-sea there sits a wasted land," Said he thereafterward, "whose name is Crete, Under whose king the world of old was chaste.	"In the mid-sea there sits a wasted land," He said, "Whose name is Crete, Under whose king the old world was chaste.
There is a mountain there, that once was glad With waters and with leaves, which was called Ida; Now 'tis deserted, as a thing worn out.	There is a mountain there that was once glad With waters and leaves, which was called Ida; Now it is deserted, a worn out thing.
Rhea once chose it for the faithful cradle Of her own son; and to conceal him better, Whene'er he cried, she there had clamours made.	Rhea once chose it for the faithful cradle Of her own son; and to conceal him Whenever he cried, she made loud clamors there.

A grand old man stands in the mount erect,
Who holds his shoulders turned tow'rds Damietta,
And looks at Rome as if it were his mirror.

His head is fashioned of refined gold,
And of pure silver are the arms and breast;
Then he is brass as far down as the fork.

From that point downward all is chosen iron,
Save that the right foot is of kiln-baked clay,
And more he stands on that than on the other.

Each part, except the gold, is by a fissure
Asunder cleft, that dripping is with tears,
Which gathered together perforate that cavern.

From rock to rock they fall into this valley;
Acheron, Styx, and Phlegethon they form;
Then downward go along this narrow sluice

Unto that point where is no more descending.
They form Cocytus; what that pool may be
Thou shalt behold, so here 'tis not narrated."

And I to him: "If so the present runnel
Doth take its rise in this way from our world,
Why only on this verge appears it to us?"

And he to me: "Thou knowest the place is round,
And notwithstanding thou hast journeyed far,
Still to the left descending to the bottom,

Thou hast not yet through all the circle turned.
Therefore if something new appear to us,
It should not bring amazement to thy face."

And I again: "Master, where shall be found
Lethe and Phlegethon, for of one thou'rt silent,

And sayest the other of this rain is made?"

"In all thy questions truly thou dost please me,"
Replied he; "but the boiling of the red
Water might well solve one of them thou makest.

Thou shalt see Lethe, but outside this moat,
There where the souls repair to lave themselves,

A grand old man stands erect in the mount,
Who holds his shoulders turned towards Damietta,
And looks at Rome as if it were his mirror.

His head is fashioned of refined gold,
And his arms and breast are of pure silver;
Then he is brass as far down as the fork.

From that point downward all is iron,
Except the right foot which is baked clay,
Upon which he stands more than the other.

Each part, except the gold, is cleft by a fissure
That drips with tears,
Which gather together and perforate that cavern.

From rock to rock they fall into this valley;
Acheron, Styx, and Phlegethon are formed;
And go downward along this narrow sluice

To the point where there is no more descending.
They form Cocytus; the pool you may
See, so it is not narrated."

I replied: "If the present river
Takes its rise from our world this way,
Why does this part appear to us?"

He said to me: "You know the place is round,
And not including what you have already seen,
You still have to descend to the bottom,

Through all the circles.
Therefore if something new appears to us,
It should not amaze you."

And I said to him: "Master, where shall we find
Lethe and Phlegethon, for one you have said
nothing,
And the other you said is made of rain?"

"In all your questions you truly please me,"
He replied; "But the boiling of the red
Water might solve one of your questions.

You will see Lethe, but outside this moat,
Where the souls prepare to wash themselves,

When sin repented of has been removed."

Then said he: "It is time now to abandon
The wood; take heed that thou come after me;
A way the margins make that are not burning,

And over them all vapours are extinguished."

When repented sin has been removed."

Then he said: "It is time now to abandon
The wood; Take heed that you come after me;
There is a way the margins make that are not
burning,
And all the vapors over them are extinguished."

Inferno: Canto XV

Now bears us onward one of the hard margins,
And so the brooklet's mist o'ershadows it,
From fire it saves the water and the dikes.

Even as the Flemings, 'twixt Cadsand and Bruges,
Fearing the flood that tow'rds them hurls itself,
Their bulwarks build to put the sea to flight;

And as the Paduans along the Brenta,
To guard their villas and their villages,
Or ever Chiarentana feel the heat;

In such similitude had those been made,
Albeit not so lofty nor so thick,
Whoever he might be, the master made them.

Now were we from the forest so remote,
I could not have discovered where it was,
Even if backward I had turned myself,

When we a company of souls encountered,
Who came beside the dike, and every one
Gazed at us, as at evening we are wont

To eye each other under a new moon,
And so towards us sharpened they their brows
As an old tailor at the needle's eye.

Thus scrutinised by such a family,
By some one I was recognised, who seized
My garment's hem, and cried out, "What a marvel!"

And I, when he stretched forth his arm to me,
On his baked aspect fastened so mine eyes,
That the scorched countenance prevented not

His recognition by my intellect;
And bowing down my face unto his own,
I made reply, "Are you here, Ser Brunetto?"

And he: "May't not displease thee, O my son,
If a brief space with thee Brunetto Latini

Now we bore on one of the hard margins,
With the brook's mist overshadowing it,
Saving the water and the dikes from fire.

Like the Flemings, between Cadsand and Bruges,
Fearing the flood that hurled itself towards them,
Built the bulwarks to put the sea to flight;

And as the Paduans along the Brenta,
In effort to guard their villas and their villages,
Or ever Chiarentana feel the heat;

In such similar ways had those been made,
Although not so high or thick,
They were made by the master.

Now we were so remote from the forest,
I could not have discovered where it was,
Even if I had turned myself backwards,

When we encountered a company of souls,
Who came beside the dike, and
Gazed at us, as we are accustomed to

Look at each other under a new moon,
And so they sharpened their brows towards us
Like an old tailor at the eye of a needle.

Thus scrutinized by each family,
I was recognized by one, who seized
My garment's hem, and cried out, "What a
marvel!"
And I, when he stretched out his arm to me,
Looked upon his baked aspect,
That the scorched countenance did not prevent

Recognition by my intellect;
And bowing down to meet his face,
I replied: "Are you here, Sir Brunetto?"

He said: "Do not be displeased, my son,
If after a brief time with you, Brunetto Latini,

Backward return and let the trail go on."

I said to him: "With all my power I ask it;
And if you wish me to sit down with you,
I will, if he please, for I go with him."

"O son," he said, "whoever of this herd
A moment stops, lies then a hundred years,

Nor fans himself when smiteth him the fire.

Therefore go on; I at thy skirts will come,
And afterward will I rejoin my band,
Which goes lamenting its eternal doom."

I did not dare to go down from the road
Level to walk with him; but my head bowed
I held as one who goeth reverently.

And he began: "What fortune or what fate
Before the last day leadeth thee down here?
And who is this that showeth thee the way?"

"Up there above us in the life serene,"
I answered him, "I lost me in a valley,
Or ever yet my age had been completed.

But yestermorn I turned my back upon it;
This one appeared to me, returning thither,
And homeward leadeth me along this road."

And he to me: "If thou thy star do follow,
Thou canst not fail thee of a glorious port,
If well I judged in the life beautiful.

And if I had not died so prematurely,
Seeing Heaven thus benignant unto thee,
I would have given thee comfort in the work.

But that ungrateful and malignant people,
Which of old time from Fesole descended,
And smacks still of the mountain and the granite,

Will make itself, for thy good deeds, thy foe;

And it is right; for among crabbed sorbs
It ill befits the sweet fig to bear fruit.

Turned backwards and let the trail go on."

I said to him: "With all my power I ask;
If you wish me to sit down with you,
I will ask him, whom I follow."

"Oh son," he said, "Whoever in this herd
Stops for a moment, must lie then for a hundred years,
And fan himself when smitten by fire.

Therefore go on; I will come after you,
And then I will rejoin my band,
Which goes lamenting its eternal doom."

I did not dare to go down from the road
To walk level with him; but bowing my head
I went as one in reverence.

And he began: "What fortune or fate
Before your last day led you down here?
And who is this that shows you the way?"

"Up there above us in the serene life,"
I answered him, "I got lost in a valley,
Before my age had been completed.

But yesterday morning I turned my back upon life;
This one appeared to me, returning here,
And led me homeward along this road."

He replied: "If you follow that star,
You cannot fail to find a glorious port,
If I judged you well in the beautiful life.

And if I had not died so prematurely,
Seeing how kind Heaven is to you,
I would have given you comfort in the work.

But that ungrateful and malignant people,
Which descended from the old time of Fesole,
And smacks still of the mountain and the granite,

Will make itself your foe because of your good deeds;
And it goes; for among the crabbed sorb tree
It bears a grudge against the sweet fig to bear fruit.

Old rumour in the world proclaims them blind;
A people avaricious, envious, proud;

Take heed that of their customs thou do cleanse thee.

Thy fortune so much honour doth reserve thee,
One party and the other shall be hungry
For thee; but far from goat shall be the grass.

Their litter let the beasts of Fesole
Make of themselves, nor let them touch the plant,
If any still upon their dunghill rise,

In which may yet revive the consecrated
Seed of those Romans, who remained there when
The nest of such great malice it became."

"If my entreaty wholly were fulfilled,"
Replied I to him, "not yet would you be
In banishment from human nature placed;

For in my mind is fixed, and touches now
My heart the dear and good paternal image
Of you, when in the world from hour to hour

You taught me how a man becomes eternal;
And how much I am grateful, while I live
Behoves that in my language be discerned.

What you narrate of my career I write,
And keep it to be glossed with other text
By a Lady who can do it, if I reach her.

This much will I have manifest to you;
Provided that my conscience do not chide me,
For whatsoever Fortune I am ready.

Such handsel is not new unto mine ears;
Therefore let Fortune turn her wheel around
As it may please her, and the churl his mattock."

My Master thereupon on his right cheek
Did backward turn himself, and looked at me;
Then said: "He listeneth well who noteth it."

Nor speaking less on that account, I go
With Ser Brunetto, and I ask who are
His most known and most eminent companions.

Old rumor in the world proclaims them blind;
An avaricious, envious, and proud group of
people;
Take heed of their customs and avoid them.

Your fortune reserves much honor for you,
However, one party or the other will be hungry
For you; but the grass will be far from the goat.

Their descendants let the beasts of Fesole
Procreate, but not touch the plant,
If any still survive,

In which may revive the consecrated
Seed of those Romans, who remained there when
It became the nest of such great malice."

"If my entreaty were wholly fulfilled,"
I replied to him, "You would not yet be
In banishment from the place of human nature;

For in my mind, and in my heart
I remember a dear and good paternal image
Of you, when in the world from morning to night

You taught me how a man becomes eternal;
And I am grateful, while I live
That I am behooved to know the language.

What you say of my career I write,
And keep it to be combined with other text
By a Lady who can do it, if I reach her.

This much I will manifest to you;
Provided that my conscience does not chide me,
For whatsoever Fortune has in store for me.

Such tokens of good fortune are not new to me;
Therefore let Fortune turn her wheel around
As she pleases and the peasant his blade."

My master upon his right cheek
Turned himself backwards and looked at me;
Then said: "He who listens well will take note."

Not speaking on that account, I went
With Sir Brunetto, and asked who were
His most known and eminent companions.

And he to me: "To know of some is well;
Of others it were laudable to be silent,
For short would be the time for so much speech.

Know them in sum, that all of them were clerks,
And men of letters great and of great fame,
In the world tainted with the selfsame sin.
Priscian goes yonder with that wretched crowd,
And Francis of Accorso; and thou hadst seen there

If thou hadst had a hankering for such scurf,

That one, who by the Servant of the Servants
From Arno was transferred to Bacchiglione,
Where he has left his sin-excited nerves.

More would I say, but coming and discoursing
Can be no longer; for that I behold
New smoke uprising yonder from the sand.

A people comes with whom I may not be;

Commended unto thee be my Tesoro,
In which I still live, and no more I ask."

Then he turned round, and seemed to be of those
Who at Verona run for the Green Mantle
Across the plain; and seemed to be among the

The one who wins, and not the one who loses.

He said to me: "To know of some is okay;
But it is best to be silent about others,
For I do not have much time to speak.

Know that many were clergymen,
And scholars and famous men,
Tainted in the world with the same selfish sin.
Priscian goes yonder with that wretched crowd,
And Francis of Accorso; and you would have seen there
If you had known such trash,

That one, who by the Servant of the Servants
From Arno was transferred to Bacchiglione,
Where he left his nerves excited by sin.

I would say more, but I cannot talk
Any longer; For I see
New smoke rising up from the sand over there.

Meaning a people is coming with whom I may not be;
Commend me to my Tesoro,
While you still live and I ask no more."

Then he turned around and seemed to be of those
Who run for the Green Mantle at Verona
Across the plain; And he seemed to be among them
Who wins and not the ones who lose.

Inferno: Canto XVI

Now was I where was heard the reverberation Of water falling into the next round, Like to that humming which the beehives make,	Now I was where I heard the reverberation Of falling water into the next round, Like the humming made by a beehive,
When shadows three together started forth, Running, from out a company that passed Beneath the rain of the sharp martyrdom.	When three shadows started forth together, Running, from out of a passing company Beneath the rain of sharp martyrdom.
Towards us came they, and each one cried out: "Stop, thou; for by thy garb to us thou seemest To be some one of our depraved city."	They came towards us crying: "Stop, you; for by your clothes you seem To be someone from our depraved city."
Ah me! what wounds I saw upon their limbs,	Ah me! What wounds I saw upon their arms and legs,
Recent and ancient by the flames burnt in! It pains me still but to remember it.	Both recent and old, by the flames burning within! It pains me to remember it still.
Unto their cries my Teacher paused attentive;	In response to their cries, my Teacher paused attentively;
He turned his face towards me, and "Now wait,"	He turned his face towards me, and said: "Now wait.
He said; "to these we should be courteous.	We should be courteous to those.
And if it were not for the fire that darts The nature of this region, I should say That haste were more becoming thee than them."	And if it were not for the fire that darts In this region, I would say That haste would be more becoming to you than them."
As soon as we stood still, they recommenced The old refrain, and when they overtook us, Formed of themselves a wheel, all three of them.	As soon as we stood still, they recommenced The old refrain, and they overtook us, They formed a wheel together.
As champions stripped and oiled are wont to do,	As champions, stripped and oiled, are used to doing,
Watching for their advantage and their hold, Before they come to blows and thrusts between them,	Watching for their advantage and their hold, Before they begin to fight,
Thus, wheeling round, did every one his visage Direct to me, so that in opposite wise His neck and feet continual journey made.	Thus the wheeling around of the men began Staring at me, so that the only movement was Their neck and feet as they continually made their journey.
And, "If the misery of this soft place	And, "If the misery of this soft place

Bring in disdain ourselves and our entreaties,"

Began one, "and our aspect black and blistered,

Let the renown of us thy mind incline
To tell us who thou art, who thus securely
Thy living feet dost move along through Hell.

He in whose footprints thou dost see me treading,
Naked and skinless though he now may go,
Was of a greater rank than thou dost think;

He was the grandson of the good Gualdrada;
His name was Guidoguerra, and in life
Much did he with his wisdom and his sword.

The other, who close by me treads the sand,
Tegghiaio Aldobrandi is, whose fame
Above there in the world should welcome be.

And I, who with them on the cross am placed,
Jacopo Rusticucci was; and truly
My savage wife, more than aught else, doth harm me."

Could I have been protected from the fire,
Below I should have thrown myself among them,
And think the Teacher would have suffered it;

But as I should have burned and baked myself,
My terror overmastered my good will,
Which made me greedy of embracing them.

Then I began: "Sorrow and not disdain
Did your condition fix within me so,
That tardily it wholly is stripped off,

As soon as this my Lord said unto me
Words, on account of which I thought within me
That people such as you are were approaching.

I of your city am; and evermore
Your labours and your honourable names
I with affection have retraced and heard.

I leave the gall, and go for the sweet fruits
Promised to me by the veracious Leader;
But to the centre first I needs must plunge."

Bring about disdain among ourselves and our guests,"
One began, "And our black and blistered appearance,
Incline your mind to remember us, then
Tell us who you are, who walks securely about
On living feet through Hell.

He in whose footprints you see me treading,
Naked and skinless as he is now
Was of greater rank than you may think;

He was the grandson of the good Gualdrada;
His name was Guidoguerra, and in life
He did much with his wisdom and his sword.

The other who treads close by me in the sand,
Is Tegghiaio Aldobrandi, whose fame
Above in the world should be welcome.

And I, who am placed on the cross with them,
Was Jacopo Rusticucci; and truly
My savage wife, more than anyone else, harmed me."
Could I have been protected from the fire,
Below I would have thrown myself among them,
And think the Teacher would have suffered it;

But as I would have burned and baked,
My terror overmastered my good will,
Which made me greedy for wanting to embrace them.
Then I began: "Sorrow and not disdain
Fixed your condition within me so,
That it is completely stripped off."

As soon as this was said my Lord told me
Something, because of what I thought
Of the people who were approaching.

"I am of your city and evermore
Your labors and honorable names
I have heard and retraced with affection.

I leave the gall, and go for the sweet fruits
Promised to me by the veracious Leader;
But I must first plunge to the center."

"So may the soul for a long while conduct
Those limbs of thine," did he make answer then,
"And so may thy renown shine after thee,

Valour and courtesy, say if they dwell
Within our city, as they used to do,
Or if they wholly have gone out of it;

For Guglielmo Borsier, who is in torment
With us of late, and goes there with his comrades,
Doth greatly mortify us with his words."

"The new inhabitants and the sudden gains

Pride and extravagance have in thee engendered,
Florence, so that thou weep'st thereat already!"

In this wise I exclaimed with face uplifted;
And the three, taking that for my reply,
Looked at each other, as one looks at truth.

"If other times so little it doth cost thee,"
Replied they all, "to satisfy another,
Happy art thou, thus speaking at thy will!

Therefore, if thou escape from these dark places,
And come to rebehold the beauteous stars,
When it shall pleasure thee to say, 'I was,'

See that thou speak of us unto the people."
Then they broke up the wheel, and in their flight
It seemed as if their agile legs were wings.

Not an Amen could possibly be said
So rapidly as they had disappeared;
Wherefore the Master deemed best to depart.

I followed him, and little had we gone,
Before the sound of water was so near us,
That speaking we should hardly have been heard.

Even as that stream which holdeth its own course
The first from Monte Veso tow'rds the East,
Upon the left-hand slope of Apennine,

Which is above called Acquacheta, ere
It down descendeth into its low bed,
And at Forli is vacant of that name,

"May your soul conduct for a long while
Those limbs of yours," he said,
"And so may your renown shine after you.

Do valor and courtesy, still dwell
Within our city, as they used to,
Or have they gone completely?

For Guglielm Borsier, who is in Torment
With us lately, and goes there with his comrades,
Greatly mortifies us with his words."

"The new inhabitants and the sudden development
of
Pride and extravagance have taken over
Florence, so that you would already weep!"

With this proclamation I uplifted my face;
And the three, accepting my reply,
Looked at each other as seeing the truth.

"If it doesn't cost you anything,"
They replied, "To satisfy another question,
And it makes you happy, please speak at your will!

So, if you escape these dark places,
And again see the beautiful stars,
You may say, 'I was here'

See that you speak of us to people."
Then they broke up the wheel and in leaving
It seemed as if their legs were wings.

An amen could not even be said,
They disappeared so rapidly;
When the Master said it best to depart.

I followed him and we had not gone very far,
Before I heard the sound of water so near us,
That we could hardly hear ourselves talk.

Like the stream which holds its own course
From the Monte Veso towards the East,
Upon the left-hand slope of Apennine,

Which is called Acquacheta,
Descending down into its low bed,
And losing its name at Forli

Reverberates there above San Benedetto From Alps, by falling at a single leap, Where for a thousand there were room enough;	*Reverberating there above San Benedetto* *From the Alps, by falling at a single leap,* *Where there is enough room for a thousand;*
Thus downward from a bank precipitate, We found resounding that dark-tinted water, So that it soon the ear would have offended.	*We found resounding a dark-tinted water* *Falling downward from a bank precipice,* *Offending the ear.*
I had a cord around about me girt, And therewithal I whilom had designed To take the panther with the painted skin.	*I had a cord around my waist,* *That I had formally designed* *To kill the panther with the painted skin.*
After I this had all from me unloosed, As my Conductor had commanded me, I reached it to him, gathered up and coiled,	*After I had loosened it,* *As commanded by my Conductor,* *I gave it to him gathered and coiled,*
Whereat he turned himself to the right side, And at a little distance from the verge, He cast it down into that deep abyss.	*Where he turned himself to the right side,* *And at little distance from the edge,* *He cast it down into the deep abyss.*
"It must needs be some novelty respond," I said within myself, "to the new signal The Master with his eye is following so."	*"It must be the need of some new response,"* *I said to myself, "To the new signal* *That the Master is following with his eye."*
Ah me! how very cautious men should be With those who not alone behold the act, But with their wisdom look into the thoughts!	*Ah me! How very cautious men should be* *With those who not only behold the act,* *But look into men's thoughts!*
He said to me: "Soon there will upward come	*He said to me: "Soon something will come* *upward so*
What I await; and what thy thought is dreaming Must soon reveal itself unto thy sight."	*I await; and what you took as a dream* *Will soon reveal itself."*
Aye to that truth which has the face of falsehood, A man should close his lips as far as may be, Because without his fault it causes shame;	*To the unseeming truth,* *A man should close his lips,* *Because without fault he causes shame;*
But here I cannot; and, Reader, by the notes Of this my Comedy to thee I swear, So may they not be void of lasting favour,	*But here I cannot; and Reader, by the notes* *Of my Comedy I swear to you,* *So they may not be void of lasting favor*
Athwart that dense and darksome atmosphere I saw a figure swimming upward come, Marvellous unto every steadfast heart,	*Amidst that dense and dark place* *I saw a figure swimming upward* *Marveling in my steadfast heart,*
Even as he returns who goeth down	*Like one, who must return after going down*

Sometimes to clear an anchor, which has grappled	*Sometimes to rid an anchor, which has become hung on a*
Reef, or aught else that in the sea is hidden,	*Reef, or something else hidden in the sea,*
Who upward stretches, and draws in his feet.	*Who stretches upward and draws his feet.*

Inferno: Canto XVII

"Behold the monster with the pointed tail,
Who cleaves the hills, and breaketh walls and weapons,

Behold him who infecteth all the world."

Thus unto me my Guide began to say,
And beckoned him that he should come to shore,
Near to the confine of the trodden marble;

And that uncleanly image of deceit
Came up and thrust ashore its head and bust,
But on the border did not drag its tail.

The face was as the face of a just man,
Its semblance outwardly was so benign,
And of a serpent all the trunk beside.

Two paws it had, hairy unto the armpits;
The back, and breast, and both the sides it had
Depicted o'er with nooses and with shields.

With colours more, groundwork or broidery
Never in cloth did Tartars make nor Turks,
Nor were such tissues by Arachne laid.

As sometimes wherries lie upon the shore,
That part are in the water, part on land;
And as among the guzzling Germans there,

The beaver plants himself to wage his war;
So that vile monster lay upon the border,
Which is of stone, and shutteth in the sand.

His tail was wholly quivering in the void,
Contorting upwards the envenomed fork,

That in the guise of scorpion armed its point.

The Guide said: "Now perforce must turn aside
Our way a little, even to that beast
Malevolent, that yonder coucheth him."

"Behold the monster with the pointed tail,
Who cleaves to the hills, and breaks down the
walls and we aprons,
Behold he who infects all the world,"

My Guide began to say to me.
As he beckoned him to come to the shore,
Near the confine of the trodden marble;

The unclean image of deceit
Came up and thrust its head and bust ashore,
But did not drag its tail on the border.

The face was of a just man;
It looked so benign,
But the trunk was like a serpent.

It had two paws leading to hairy armpits;
On both sides of his back and breast
He wore nooses and shields.

He was the color of groundwork or embroidery,
But not like the Tartars or the Turks made.
Nor did Arachne create such elements.

As sometimes boats lie upon the shore,
That are part on water and part on land
And as among the guzzling Germans

Plant themselves to wage war,
The vile monster lay upon the border,
Made of stone in the sand.

His tail was quivering in the void,
Contorting upwards revealing the envenomed
fork,
Resembling the scorpion with his armed point.

The Guide said: "Now we must turn aside
From our way just a little, to avoid that
Malevolent beast over there."

We therefore on the right side descended,
And made ten steps upon the outer verge,
Completely to avoid the sand and flame;

And after we are come to him, I see
A little farther off upon the sand
A people sitting near the hollow place.

Then said to me the Master: "So that full
Experience of this round thou bear away,
Now go and see what their condition is.

There let thy conversation be concise;
Till thou returnest I will speak with him,
That he concede to us his stalwart shoulders."

Thus farther still upon the outermost
Head of that seventh circle all alone
I went, where sat the melancholy folk.

Out of their eyes was gushing forth their woe;
This way, that way, they helped them with their hands

Now from the flames and now from the hot soil.

Not otherwise in summer do the dogs,
Now with the foot, now with the muzzle, when
By fleas, or flies, or gadflies, they are bitten.

When I had turned mine eyes upon the faces
Of some, on whom the dolorous fire is falling,
Not one of them I knew; but I perceived

That from the neck of each there hung a pouch,
Which certain colour had, and certain blazon;
And thereupon it seems their eyes are feeding.

And as I gazing round me come among them,
Upon a yellow pouch I azure saw
That had the face and posture of a lion.

Proceeding then the current of my sight,
Another of them saw I, red as blood,
Display a goose more white than butter is.

And one, who with an azure sow and gravid
Emblazoned had his little pouch of white,
Said unto me: "What dost thou in this moat?

We, therefore, descended on the right side
And made ten steps onto the outer ledge
To avoid the sand and flame completely.

After we came towards him, I saw
A little farther off upon the sand,
A people sitting near the hollow place.

Then the Master said to me: "So that you receive
The full experience of this round, go
Now and see what their condition is.

Let your conversation be concise.
I will speak with him until you return,
So he may give us a lift upon his stalwart
shoulders."
Upon the outermost
Head of that seventh circle,
I went alone where the melancholy folk sat.

Woe gushed forth out of their eyes;
They wiped them this way and that with their
hands
And fanned the flames from the hot soil.

Like dogs in the summer,
They used their feet and mouths,
To escape the bites of fleas, flies, or gadflies,

When I turned my eyes towards their faces,
On whom the dolorous fire was falling,
I did not recognize any, but I perceived

From the next of each one is a pouch
With a certain vivid color
And there it seems their eyes are feeding.

A pouch hung from the neck of each,
The yellow pouches I saw
Had the face and physique of a lion.

Then the current of my sight,
Saw another, red as blood,
Displaying a goose whiter than butter.

One, with a yellow pregnant sow
Emblazoned upon his white pouch,
Said: "What are you doing in this moat?

Now get thee gone; and since thou'rt still alive,
Know that a neighbour of mine, Vitaliano,
Will have his seat here on my left-hand side.

A Paduan am I with these Florentines;
Full many a time they thunder in mine ears,
Exclaiming, 'Come the sovereign cavalier,

He who shall bring the satchel with three goats;'"
Then twisted he his mouth, and forth he thrust
His tongue, like to an ox that licks its nose.

And fearing lest my longer stay might vex
Him who had warned me not to tarry long,
Backward I turned me from those weary souls.

I found my Guide, who had already mounted
Upon the back of that wild animal,
And said to me: "Now be both strong and bold.

Now we descend by stairways such as these;
Mount thou in front, for I will be midway,
So that the tail may have no power to harm thee."

Such as he is who has so near the ague
Of quartan that his nails are blue already,
And trembles all, but looking at the shade;

Even such became I at those proffered words;
But shame in me his menaces produced,
Which maketh servant strong before good master.

I seated me upon those monstrous shoulders;
I wished to say, and yet the voice came not
As I believed, "Take heed that thou embrace me."

But he, who other times had rescued me
In other peril, soon as I had mounted,
Within his arms encircled and sustained me,

And said: "Now, Geryon, bestir thyself;
The circles large, and the descent be little;

Think of the novel burden which thou hast."

Even as the little vessel shoves from shore,
Backward, still backward, so he thence withdrew;

Get away, since you are still alive,
And know that a neighbor of mine, Vitaliano,
Will have his seat here on my left-hand side.

I was Paduan with these Florentines,
Who so many times thundered in my ears,
Exclaiming, 'Come the sovereign cavalier,

Who shall bring the satchel with three goats,'
Then he twisted his mouth and thrust forth
His tongue, like an ox licking its nose.

And fearing my staying longer might vex
Him, who had warned me not to tarry long,
I turned backwards from those weary souls.

I found my Guide, already mounted onto
The back of that wild animal,
Who said to me: "Now be strong and bold.

For we must descend the stairways like this.
Mount in front of me, so I may be between you
And that powerful tail, and you will not be
harmed.
Like one who is sick so often
His nails turn blue,
Everything making him tremble, I looked at the
shade
And became ill at those proffered words,
But due to shame,
Which makes the servant strong before the good
master,
I seated myself upon those monstrous shoulders.
I wished to say, but my voice would not come,
"Make sure you embrace me."

But the one who had rescued me
From peril, as soon as I had mounted,
Encircled me with his arms and sustained me,

Saying: "Now, Geryon, go ahead;
Through the large circles and let the descent be
little.
Think of the new burden you carry."

Like a little vessel shoves from the shore,
He strode backwards until

And when he wholly felt himself afloat,

Feeling himself fully afloat,

There where his breast had been he turned his tail,
And that extended like an eel he moved,
And with his paws drew to himself the air.

He turned his tail where his breast had been
And extended like an eel moving
With his paws and drawing himself to the air.

A greater fear I do not think there was
What time abandoned Phaeton the reins,
Whereby the heavens, as still appears, were scorched;

I did not know of a greater fear like
When time abandoned Phaeton
Whose scorched image still appears in the
heavens,

Nor when the wretched Icarus his flanks
Felt stripped of feathers by the melting wax,
His father crying, "An ill way thou takest!"

Or when the wretched Icarus
Lost his feathers by the melting wax,
His father crying, "You have taken an ill way!"

Than was my own, when I perceived myself
On all sides in the air, and saw extinguished
The sight of everything but of the monster.

Than my own when I perceived myself
Surrounded by air and lost
Sight of everything but the monster.

Onward he goeth, swimming slowly, slowly;

Onward he went, swimming and descending
slowly

Wheels and descends, but I perceive it only
By wind upon my face and from below.

Which I perceived only
By the wind on my face from below.

I heard already on the right the whirlpool
Making a horrible crashing under us;
Whence I thrust out my head with eyes cast downward.

I heard on the right a whirlpool
Making a horrible crashing sound underneath us,
So I looked downward.

Then was I still more fearful of the abyss;
Because I fires beheld, and heard laments,
Whereat I, trembling, all the closer cling.

Then I was still more fearful of the abyss,
Because I saw fires and heard laments
Which made me tremble and cling closer.

I saw then, for before I had not seen it,
The turning and descending, by great horrors
That were approaching upon divers sides.

I saw then something I had never seen before;
The turning and descending by great horrors
Approaching upon the diver's sides.

As falcon who has long been on the wing,
Who, without seeing either lure or bird,
Maketh the falconer say, "Ah me, thou stoopest,"

Like a falcon, who has been flying
And without seeing a lure or a bird,
Makes the falconer say, "Ah me, you are low,"

Descendeth weary, whence he started swiftly,
Thorough a hundred circles, and alights
Far from his master, sullen and disdainful;

Descends wearily
Through a hundred circles and alights
Far from his master, sullen and disdainful,

Even thus did Geryon place us on the bottom,
Close to the bases of the rough-hewn rock,
And being disencumbered of our persons,

Geryon placed us on the bottom
Close to the bases of the rough-hewn rock,
After we disembarked,

He sped away as arrow from the string.

He sped away like an arrow from the string.

Inferno: Canto XVIII

There is a place in Hell called Malebolge,	*There is a place in Hell called Malebolge,*
Wholly of stone and of an iron colour,	*Which is the color of iron and made completely of*
	stone,
As is the circle that around it turns.	*Like the circle that it turns around.*
Right in the middle of the field malign	*Right in the middle of the sad field*
There yawns a well exceeding wide and deep,	*A well opened exceedingly wide and deep,*
Of which its place the structure will recount.	*The most memorable part of the structure.*
Round, then, is that enclosure which remains	*The enclosure which remained*
Between the well and foot of the high, hard bank,	*Between the well and the foot of the high, hard*
	bank, was round
And has distinct in valleys ten its bottom.	*And had ten distinct valleys in its bottom.*
As where for the protection of the walls	*For the protection of the walls,*
Many and many moats surround the castles,	*Many, many moats surrounded the castles,*
The part in which they are a figure forms,	*Forming a figure*
Just such an image those presented there;	*Like an image there.*
And as about such strongholds from their gates	*And, like such strongholds have*
Unto the outer bank are little bridges,	*Little bridges extending from their gates,*
So from the precipice's base did crags	*The crags of the precipice's base*
Project, which intersected dikes and moats,	*Projected, intersecting dikes and moats*
Unto the well that truncates and collects them.	*Into the well that truncates and collects them.*
Within this place, down shaken from the back	*Within this place, shaken from the back*
Of Geryon, we found us; and the Poet	*Of Geryon, we found ourselves; and the Poet*
Held to the left, and I moved on behind.	*Went to the left, and I moved behind.*
Upon my right hand I beheld new anguish,	*Upon my right hand I saw a new anguish,*
New torments, and new wielders of the lash,	*New torments, and new wielders of the lash,*
Wherewith the foremost Bolgia was replete.	*Where the first Bolgia, or pouch, was located.*
Down at the bottom were the sinners naked;	*The naked sinners were down at the bottom.*
This side the middle came they facing us,	*They came towards us*
Beyond it, with us, but with greater steps;	*Beyond the middle with great steps.*
Even as the Romans, for the mighty host,	*Like the Romans for the mighty host,*
The year of Jubilee, upon the bridge,	*During the year of Jubilee*
Have chosen a mode to pass the people over;	*Chose a way to pass over the people on the bridge,*

For all upon one side towards the Castle Their faces have, and go unto St. Peter's; On the other side they go towards the Mountain.	*All upon one side went towards the Castle* *Unto St. Peter's.* *On the other side they went towards the Mountain.*
This side and that, along the livid stone Beheld I horned demons with great scourges, Who cruelly were beating them behind.	*Along the livid stone,* *I beheld horned demons with great scourges,* *Who cruelly beat them from behind.*
Ah me! how they did make them lift their legs At the first blows! and sooth not any one The second waited for, nor for the third	*Ah me! How they did make them lift their legs* *With the first blows! And without soothing,* *On went the second, then the third.*
While I was going on, mine eyes by one Encountered were; and straight I said: "Already With sight of this one I am not unfed."	*While I was watching, I* *Encountered one and said:* *"I am not unfed with the sighting of this one."*
Therefore I stayed my feet to make him out, And with me the sweet Guide came to a stand, And to my going somewhat back assented;	*Therefore, I turned to make him out,* *With my sweet Guide beside me* *Assenting to my going somewhat backwards.*
And he, the scourged one, thought to hide himself, Lowering his face, but little it availed him; For said I: "Thou that castest down thine eyes,	*The scourged one, thought to hide himself,* *Lowering his face, but to little avail* *For I said: "You with the downcast eyes,*
If false are not the features which thou bearest, Thou art Venedico Caccianimico; But what doth bring thee to such pungent sauces?"	*If I am right you are* *Venedico Caccianimico,* *But what brings you to such suffering?"*
And he to me: "Unwillingly I tell it; But forces me thine utterance distinct, Which makes me recollect the ancient world.	*He said: "I will tell you, although unwillingly,* *With distinct language,* *Which makes me think of the ancient world.*
I was the one who the fair Ghisola Induced to grant the wishes of the Marquis, Howe'er the shameless story may be told.	*I was the one who fair Ghisola* *Bed to grant the wishes of the marquis,* *However shameless the story may be told.*
Not the sole Bolognese am I who weeps here; Nay, rather is this place so full of them, That not so many tongues to-day are taught	*I am not the only Bolognese who weeps here.* *Rather this place is so full of them,* *That there aren't as many students taught today.*
'Twixt Reno and Savena to say 'sipa;' And if thereof thou wishest pledge or proof, Bring to thy mind our avaricious heart."	*Between Reno and Savena, to say, 'sipa;'* *And if you wish for a pledge or proof,* *Remember our avaricious heart."*
While speaking in this manner, with his scourge A demon smote him, and said: "Get thee gone Pander, there are no women here for coin."	*While he was speaking in this manner,* *A demon smote him and said: "Get gone* *Pander; There are no women here for sale."*

I joined myself again unto mine Escort; Thereafterward with footsteps few we came To where a crag projected from the bank.	*I joined my Escort again;* *Where we shortly came* *To where a crag projected from the bank.*
This very easily did we ascend, And turning to the right along its ridge, From those eternal circles we departed.	*We easily ascended,* *And turning to the right along its ridge,* *We departed from those eternal circles.*
When we were there, where it is hollowed out Beneath, to give a passage to the scourged, The Guide said: "Wait, and see that on thee strike	*When we were where it was hollowed out,* *To give passage to the scourged,* *The Guide said: "Wait, and see on the strike*
The vision of those others evil-born, Of whom thou hast not yet beheld the faces, Because together with us they have gone."	*The image of these sinners,* *Whose faces you have not seen* *Because they fled from us.*
From the old bridge we looked upon the train Which tow'rds us came upon the other border, And which the scourges in like manner smite.	*From the old bridge we looked upon the train* *Which came towards us on the other side,* *Which came towards us on the other side,*
And the good Master, without my inquiring, Said to me: "See that tall one who is coming, And for his pain seems not to shed a tear;	*And the good Master, without my asking,* *Said to me: "See the tall one who is coming,* *Who does not shed a tear from his pain?*
Still what a royal aspect he retains! That Jason is, who by his heart and cunning The Colchians of the Ram made destitute.	*He retains his royal aspect!* *That is Jason, who by his heart and cunning* *Made the Colchians of the Ram destitute.*
He by the isle of Lemnos passed along After the daring women pitiless Had unto death devoted all their males.	*He passed by the isle of Lemnos* *After the daring women without pity* *Devoted all their males to death.*
There with his tokens and with ornate words Did he deceive Hypsipyle, the maiden Who first, herself, had all the rest deceived.	*There with his tokens and ornate words* *He deceived Hypsipyle,* *The maiden, who, at first, had all the rest deceived.*
There did he leave her pregnant and forlorn; Such sin unto such punishment condemns him, And also for Medea is vengeance done.	*He left her pregnant and forlorn* *Condemning him unto such punishment, and* *Giving Medea vengeance.*
With him go those who in such wise deceive; And this sufficient be of the first valley	*Those who share his wise deceit go with him.* *This should be sufficient information of the first valley*
To know, and those that in its jaws it holds."	*For you to know of those within its jaws."*
We were already where the narrow path Crosses athwart the second dike, and forms Of that a buttress for another arch.	*We were already where the narrow path* *Crossed the second dike and formed* *A buttress for another arch.*

Thence we heard people, who are making moan
In the next Bolgia, snorting with their muzzles,
And with their palms beating upon themselves

The margins were incrusted with a mould
By exhalation from below, that sticks there,
And with the eyes and nostrils wages war.

The bottom is so deep, no place suffices
To give us sight of it, without ascending
The arch's back, where most the crag impends.

Thither we came, and thence down in the moat
I saw a people smothered in a filth
That out of human privies seemed to flow;

And whilst below there with mine eye I search,
I saw one with his head so foul with ordure,
It was not clear if he were clerk or layman.

He screamed to me: "Wherefore art thou so eager
To look at me more than the other foul ones?"
And I to him: "Because, if I remember,

I have already seen thee with dry hair,
And thou'rt Alessio Interminei of Lucca;
Therefore I eye thee more than all the others."

And he thereon, belabouring his pumpkin:
"The flatteries have submerged me here below,
Wherewith my tongue was never surfeited."

Then said to me the Guide: "See that thou thrust
Thy visage somewhat farther in advance,
That with thine eyes thou well the face attain

Of that uncleanly and dishevelled drab,
Who there doth scratch herself with filthy nails,
And crouches now, and now on foot is standing.

Thais the harlot is it, who replied
Unto her paramour, when he said, 'Have I

Great gratitude from thee?'--'Nay, marvellous;'

And herewith let our sight be satisfied."

We heard people, in the next Bolgia
Moaning and Snorting with their muzzles,
And beating themselves with their palms.

The margins were incrusted with mold
Sticking there
Waging war on the eyes and nostrils.

The bottom was so deep, no place sufficed
To give us sight of it, without ascending
The back of the arch where the crag jutted out the
most.
So we went up and down into the moat,
Where I saw people smothered in filth
That seemed to flow from human privates.

While there, I searched below with my eye
And saw one with his head so foul with odor,
It was not clear if he were a clergyman or a
layman.
He screamed to me: "Why are you so eager
To look at me more than the other foul ones?"
To which I replied: "Because, if I remember,

I have already seen you with dry hair.
You are Alessio Interminei of Lucca;
Therefore, I look at you more than the rest."

He went on laboring with his pumpkin:
"The flatterers have submerged me here below,
Where my tongue was not sufficient."

Then my Guide said: "See that you look
Farther away,
So you may attain the face

Of that unclean and disheveled drab,
Who scratches herself with filthy nails
And crouches one minute and stands the next.

It is Thais the harlot, who replied
To her paramour when he said, 'Have I great
gratitude from you?'
'No, marvelous.'

And with that, let your look be satisfied."

Inferno: Canto XIX

O Simon Magus, O forlorn disciples,
Ye who the things of God, which ought to be
The brides of holiness, rapaciously

For silver and for gold do prostitute,
Now it behoves for you the trumpet sound,
Because in this third Bolgia ye abide.

We had already on the following tomb
Ascended to that portion of the crag
Which o'er the middle of the moat hangs plumb.

Wisdom supreme, O how great art thou showest
In heaven, in earth, and in the evil world,
And with what justice doth thy power distribute!

I saw upon the sides and on the bottom
The livid stone with perforations filled,
All of one size, and every one was round.

To me less ample seemed they not, nor greater
Than those that in my beautiful Saint John
Are fashioned for the place of the baptisers,

And one of which, not many years ago,
I broke for some one, who was drowning in it;
Be this a seal all men to undeceive.

Out of the mouth of each one there protruded
The feet of a transgressor, and the legs
Up to the calf, the rest within remained.

In all of them the soles were both on fire;
Wherefore the joints so violently quivered,
They would have snapped asunder withes and bands.

Even as the flame of unctuous things is wont
To move upon the outer surface only,
So likewise was it there from heel to point.

"Master, who is that one who writhes himself,
More than his other comrades quivering,"

Oh Simon Magus, Oh forlorn disciples,
You who the things of God, which should be
The brides of holiness, with fervor

For silver and gold prostitute.
Now the sound of the trumpet behooves you
Because you live in this third Bolgia.

We had already on the next tomb
Ascended to that portion of the crag
Which hung over plumb with the middle of the
moat.
Supreme wisdom, Oh how great you show
In heaven, in earth, and in the evil world,
And what justice you powerfully distribute!

I saw upon the sides and on the bottom
The livid stone filled with round perforations
Of one size.

To me, they did not seem less ample or greater
Than those that my beautiful Saint John
Was fashioned for the place of the baptizers,

And one, which many years ago,
I broke for someone, who was drowning in it;
This was a seal to deceitful men.

Protruding out of the mouth of each one was
The feet of a transgressor, and the legs,
Up to the calf, remained within the rest.

In all of them the soles were both on fire,
Making the joints quiver so violently
They would have snapped.

Even as the flame of unctuous thins is likely
To move up the outer surface,
So was the fire from heel to point.

"Master, who is that one who writhes himself,
More than his other comrades,"

I said, "and whom a redder flame is sucking?"

And he to me: "If thou wilt have me bear thee
Down there along that bank which lowest lies,
From him thou'lt know his errors and himself."

And I: "What pleases thee, to me is pleasing;
Thou art my Lord, and knowest that I depart not

From thy desire, and knowest what is not spoken."

Straightway upon the fourth dike we arrived;
We turned, and on the left-hand side descended
Down to the bottom full of holes and narrow.

And the good Master yet from off his haunch
Deposed me not, till to the hole he brought me
Of him who so lamented with his shanks.

"Whoe'er thou art, that standest upside down,
O doleful soul, implanted like a stake,"
To say began I, "if thou canst, speak out."

I stood even as the friar who is confessing
The false assassin, who, when he is fixed,
Recalls him, so that death may be delayed.

And he cried out: "Dost thou stand there already,
Dost thou stand there already, Boniface?
By many years the record lied to me.

Art thou so early satiate with that wealth,
For which thou didst not fear to take by fraud
The beautiful Lady, and then work her woe?"

Such I became, as people are who stand,
Not comprehending what is answered them,
As if bemocked, and know not how to answer.

Then said Virgilius: "Say to him straightway,
'I am not he, I am not he thou thinkest.'"
And I replied as was imposed on me.

Whereat the spirit writhed with both his feet,
Then, sighing, with a voice of lamentation
Said to me: "Then what wantest thou of me?

If who I am thou carest so much to know,

I said, "And who sucks a redder flame?"

*He replied: "If you will have me take you
Down there along the lowest lying bank,
You will know him and his errors."*

*I said: "Whatever pleases you, is pleasing to me.
You are my Lord, and you know that I do not
depart from
Your desire, and you know what is not spoken."*

*We went straight away to the fourth dike.
We turned and on the left side descended
Down to the narrow bottom full of holes.*

*And the Master with me by his side
Did not leave me until he brought me to the hole
Of the one who lamented with his legs.*

*"Whoever you are, that stands upside down,
Oh sad soul, implanted like a stake,"
I began to say, "if you can, speak."*

*I stood like friar who is confessing
The false assassin, when he is ill
Recalling him so that death may be delayed.*

*He cried out: "Do you stand there already,
Do you stand there already, Boniface?
The record lied to me for many years.*

*Have you already spent your wealth
For which you made by fraud
By working the beautiful Lady?"*

*I became like people who stand
Not understanding what is being said,
As if I were being mocked and did not know what
to say.
Then Virgilius said: "Tell him,
'I am not who you think I am.'"
And I did as I was told.*

*Then the spirit writhed with both of his feet,
Sighing with a voice of lamentation and said
"Then what do you want from me?*

If you care to know who I am so much,

That thou on that account hast crossed the bank,
Know that I vested was with the great mantle;

And truly was I son of the She-bear,
So eager to advance the cubs, that wealth
Above, and here myself, I pocketed.

Beneath my head the others are dragged down
Who have preceded me in simony,
Flattened along the fissure of the rock.

Below there I shall likewise fall, whenever
That one shall come who I believed thou wast,
What time the sudden question I proposed.

But longer I my feet already toast,
And here have been in this way upside down
Than he will planted stay with reddened feet;

For after him shall come of fouler deed
From tow'rds the west a Pastor without law,
Such as befits to cover him and me.

New Jason will he be, of whom we read
In Maccabees; and as his king was pliant,
So he who governs France shall be to this one."

I do not know if I were here too bold,
That him I answered only in this metre:
"I pray thee tell me now how great a treasure

Our Lord demanded of Saint Peter first,
Before he put the keys into his keeping?
Truly he nothing asked but 'Follow me.'

Nor Peter nor the rest asked of Matthias
Silver or gold, when he by lot was chosen
Unto the place the guilty soul had lost.

Therefore stay here, for thou art justly punished,

And keep safe guard o'er the ill-gotten money,
Which caused thee to be valiant against Charles.

And were it not that still forbids it me
The reverence for the keys superlative
Thou hadst in keeping in the gladsome life,

That you dared to cross the bank,
Know that I was once vested with a great mantle;

I truly was the son of the She-bear,
So eager to advance the cubs, that
I pocketed wealth above here.

Beneath me, the others are dragged down,
Who have preceded me in simony,
And been flattened along the fissure of the rock.

I shall fall below likewise, whenever
The one I mistook you for,
When I asked you the question arrives.

But my feet have already been toasted
And I have been upside down longer
Than he will stay planted with reddened feet;

For after him another will come of worse deeds
From towards the west, a pastor without law,
Who should cover him and me.

He will be Jason, of whom we read
In Maccabees; and his king was flexible,
So he thought the one who governs France would be also."

I do not know if I were too bold at this point
When I asked him:
"Please tell me how great a treasure

Our Lord demanded of Saint Peter
Before he gave him the keys to heaven?
He asked for nothing except to 'Follow me.'

Neither Peter nor the rest asked Matthias
For Silver or gold, when he was chosen by lots
To the place lost by guilty souls.

Therefore, stay here, where you are punished justly,
And keep safeguard over the ill-gotten money,
Which caused you to go against Charles.

And if it were not forbidden to speak
Against one who held the keys
You had in life,

I would make use of words more grievous still;
Because your avarice afflicts the world,
Trampling the good and lifting the depraved.

The Evangelist you Pastors had in mind,
When she who sitteth upon many waters
To fornicate with kings by him was seen;

The same who with the seven heads was born,
And power and strength from the ten horns received,

So long as virtue to her spouse was pleasing.

Ye have made yourselves a god of gold and silver;
And from the idolater how differ ye,
Save that he one, and ye a hundred worship?

Ah, Constantine! of how much ill was mother,
Not thy conversion, but that marriage dower

Which the first wealthy Father took from thee!"

And while I sang to him such notes as these,
Either that anger or that conscience stung him,
He struggled violently with both his feet.

I think in sooth that it my Leader pleased,
With such contented lip he listened ever
Unto the sound of the true words expressed.

Therefore with both his arms he took me up,
And when he had me all upon his breast,
Remounted by the way where he descended.

Nor did he tire to have me clasped to him;
But bore me to the summit of the arch
Which from the fourth dike to the fifth is passage.

There tenderly he laid his burden down,
Tenderly on the crag uneven and steep,
That would have been hard passage for the goats:

Thence was unveiled to me another valley.

I would use more grievous words;
Because your avarice afflicts the world
Trampling the good and lifting the depraved.

The Evangelism you Pastors had in mind,
When she, who sat upon many waters
To fornicate with kings, was seen by him;

Like the one who was born with seven heads,
And had the power and strength from the ten
horns received,
As long as she was virtuous to her spouse.

You have made yourself a god of gold and silver;
How are you any different from the idolater except
He worships one, and you worship a hundred?

Ah Constantine! Oh how ill was the mother,
Not by your conversion, but by the marriage
dowry
Which the first wealthy Father took from you!"

And while I sang this song to him,
Either anger or his conscience stung him so that
He struggled violently with both his feet.

I think it pleased my Leader,
For he listened contently
To the true words I expressed.

Then he took me up into both of his arms,
And when he had me upon his breast,
We took off by the way where we had descended.

He did not tire, having me clasped around him;
Instead, he bore me to the summit of the arch
Which held the passage from the fourth dike to the
fifth.
There, he laid me down tenderly
On the uneven, steep crag
That would have been hard for goats to pass;

Then another valley was unveiled to me.

Inferno: Canto XX

Of a new pain behoves me to make verses
And give material to the twentieth Canto
Of the first song, which is of the submerged.

I was already thoroughly disposed
To peer down into the uncovered depth,
Which bathed itself with tears of agony;

And people saw I through the circular valley
Silent and weeping, coming at the pace
Which in this world the Litanies assume.

As lower down my sight descended on them,
Wondrously each one seemed to be distorted
From chin to the beginning of the chest;

For tow'rds the reins the countenance was turned,
And backward it behoved them to advance,
As to look forward had been taken from them.

Perchance indeed by violence of palsy
Some one has been thus wholly turned awry;
But I ne'er saw it, nor believe it can be.

As God may let thee, Reader, gather fruit
From this thy reading, think now for thyself
How I could ever keep my face unmoistened,

When our own image near me I beheld
Distorted so, the weeping of the eyes
Along the fissure bathed the hinder parts.

Truly I wept, leaning upon a peak
Of the hard crag, so that my Escort said
To me: "Art thou, too, of the other fools?

Here pity lives when it is wholly dead;
Who is a greater reprobate than he
Who feels compassion at the doom divine?

Lift up, lift up thy head, and see for whom
Opened the earth before the Thebans' eyes;

A new pain drives me to make verses
For the twentieth Canto
Like the first song, reminiscent of the submerged.

I was already disposed
To look down into the uncovered depth,
Which bathed itself with tears of agony;

I saw people going through the circular valley,
Silent and weeping, at a pace
Assumed by the Litanies of this world.

As I looked down on them,
Each one seemed to be distorted
From the chin to the beginning of the chest;

Their heads, twisted towards the reins
Moved them backwards,
Having lost their ability to look forwards.

The product of a violent seizure
Making someone turn completely around,
I have never seen or believed it possible.

As God may let you, Reader, gather fruit
From this, and think for yourself
How could I ever keep my face dry,

When I beheld near me our own image
Distorted so that the tears from the eyes
Bathed the hind parts.

Truly, I wept, leaning upon a peak
Of the hard crag, so my Escort said
"Are you also of the other fools?

Here pity lives among the wholly dead;
Who is a greater reprobate than one,
Who feels compassion at the divine doomed?

Lift up. Lift up your head and see who
Opened the earth before the Thebans' eyes;

Wherefore they all cried: 'Whither rushest thou,	*Where they all cried: 'Why do you rush*
Amphiaraus? Why dost leave the war?' And downward ceased he not to fall amain As far as Minos, who lays hold on all. See, he has made a bosom of his shoulders! Because he wished to see too far before him Behind he looks, and backward goes his way:	*Amphiaraus? Why do you leave the war?'* *And he fell downward* *As far as Minos, who holds all.* *See, he has made a bosom of his shoulders!* *Because he wished to see too far in the future* *He looks behind him and goes backwards:*
Behold Tiresias, who his semblance changed, When from a male a female he became, His members being all of them transformed;	*Look at Tiresias, who has been changed,* *From male to female,* *All of his body parts being transformed;*
And afterwards was forced to strike once more The two entangled serpents with his rod, Ere he could have again his manly plumes.	*Afterwards, he was forced once more to strike* *The two entangled serpents with his rod,* *Before he could have his manhood back.*
That Aruns is, who backs the other's belly, Who in the hills of Luni, there where grubs The Carrarese who houses underneath,	*That is Aruns, behind the other's belly,* *Who in the hills of Luni where the* *Carrarese house the grubs underneath,*
Among the marbles white a cavern had For his abode; whence to behold the stars And sea, the view was not cut off from him.	*Made his home in the white cavern.* *Trying to interpret the stars* *And the sea.*
And she there, who is covering up her breasts, Which thou beholdest not, with loosened tresses, And on that side has all the hairy skin,	*The woman, covering up her breasts* *With her hair, and* *Has all the hairy skin on her side*
Was Manto, who made quest through many lands, Afterwards tarried there where I was born; Whereof I would thou list to me a little.	*Was Manto, who quested through many lands,* *And stayed where I was born;* *Listen to this.*
After her father had from life departed, And the city of Bacchus had become enslaved, She a long season wandered through the world.	*After her father died,* *And the city of Bacchus was enslaved,* *She wandered a long time throughout the world.*
Above in beauteous Italy lies a lake At the Alp's foot that shuts in Germany Over Tyrol, and has the name Benaco.	*Above Italy is a beautiful lake* *Shutting in Germany at the foot of the Alp's* *Over Tyrol, named Benaco.*
By a thousand springs, I think, and more, is bathed, 'Twixt Garda and Val Camonica, Pennino, With water that grows stagnant in that lake.	*Giving birth to a thousand springs,* *Between Garda, Val Camonica, and Pennino,* *The water grows stagnant.*
Midway a place is where the Trentine Pastor,	*There is a place midway where the Trentine* *Pastor,*
And he of Brescia, and the Veronese	*Of Brescia and the Veronese,*

Might give his blessing, if he passed that way.

Sitteth Peschiera, fortress fair and strong,
To front the Brescians and the Bergamasks,

Where round about the bank descendeth lowest.
There of necessity must fall whatever
In bosom of Benaco cannot stay,
And grows a river down through verdant pastures.

Soon as the water doth begin to run,
No more Benaco is it called, but Mincio,
Far as Governo, where it falls in Po.

Not far it runs before it finds a plain
In which it spreads itself, and makes it marshy,
And oft 'tis wont in summer to be sickly.

Passing that way the virgin pitiless
Land in the middle of the fen descried,
Untilled and naked of inhabitants;

There to escape all human intercourse,
She with her servants stayed, her arts to practice

And lived, and left her empty body there.

The men, thereafter, who were scattered round,
Collected in that place, which was made strong
By the lagoon it had on every side;

They built their city over those dead bones,
And, after her who first the place selected,
Mantua named it, without other omen.

Its people once within more crowded were,
Ere the stupidity of Casalodi
From Pinamonte had received deceit.

Therefore I caution thee, if e'er thou hearest
Originate my city otherwise,
No falsehood may the verity defraud."

And I: "My Master, thy discourses are
To me so certain, and so take my faith,
That unto me the rest would be spent coals.

But tell me of the people who are passing,

Might give his blessing, if he passed that way.

A strong and fair fortress, Peschiera,
Sits to the front of the Brescians and the
Bergamasks,
Where the bank is the lowest.
By necessity, whatever
In the bosom of Benaco cannot stay, falls,
And grows a river down through verdant pastures.

Where water begins to run,
It is called Minicio,
To Governo, where it runs into the Po.

It does not run far before it finds a plain,
Where it spreads and creates a marsh
And is often sickly in the summer.

Passing that way, the pitiless virgin
Land, in the middle of the fen, was
Untilled and unoccupied;

To escape contact with humans,
She stayed there with her servants to practice her
arts
Until she died.

Afterwards, men from around the land,
Collected in that place, which was made strong
By the lagoon on every side;

They built their city over her dead bones,
And after her, who first selected the place,
Named it Mantua.

Its people became overcrowded,
Before the stupidity of Casalodi
Who was deceived by Pinamonte.

Therefore, be cautious, if you ever hear
Another version of how my city originated,
And ignore the falsehood."

I said: "My Master, your version
Rings so true, in faith,
I would never believe another.

But tell me, of the people who are passing,

If any one note-worthy thou beholdest,
For only unto that my mind reverts."

Then said he to me: "He who from the cheek
Thrusts out his beard upon his swarthy shoulders
Was, at the time when Greece was void of males,

So that there scarce remained one in the cradle,
An augur, and with Calchas gave the moment,
In Aulis, when to sever the first cable.

Eryphylus his name was, and so sings
My lofty Tragedy in some part or other;
That knowest thou well, who knowest the whole of it.

The next, who is so slender in the flanks,
Was Michael Scott, who of a verity
Of magical illusions knew the game.

Behold Guido Bonatti, behold Asdente,
Who now unto his leather and his thread
Would fain have stuck, but he too late repents.

Behold the wretched ones, who left the needle,
The spool and rock, and made them fortune-tellers;
They wrought their magic spells with herb and image.

But come now, for already holds the confines
Of both the hemispheres, and under Seville
Touches the ocean-wave, Cain and the thorns,

And yesternight the moon was round already;
Thou shouldst remember well it did not harm thee
From time to time within the forest deep."

Thus spake he to me, and we walked the while.

Are any you see noteworthy,
Because I keep thinking about that."

Then he replied: "The one with
The beard to his shoulders
Was, at the time when Greece was without males,

So that there weren't any in the cradle,
An augur, and with Calchas foretold the moment,
In Aulis, when to sever the first cable.

His name was Eryphylus, and so
I sing my lofty Tragedy,
You know so well.

The next one, with the slender flanks,
Was Michael Scott, who knew
The game of magical illusions.

Look at Guido Bonatti, and Asdente,
Who would have struck his leather and thread,
But repented too late.

See the wretched ones, who left the needle,
Spool, and rock, making them fortune tellers;
They performed magic spells with herbs and
images.
But come on now, for the confines
Of both hemispheres, under Seville
Touches the ocean waves, Cain, and the thorns,

And the moon, last night, were already round;
You should remember it well; it did not harm you
Within the deep forest."

Thus, when he said this, we walked awhile.

Inferno: Canto XXI

From bridge to bridge thus, speaking other things
Of which my Comedy cares not to sing,
We came along, and held the summit, when

We halted to behold another fissure
Of Malebolge and other vain laments;
And I beheld it marvellously dark.

As in the Arsenal of the Venetians
Boils in the winter the tenacious pitch
To smear their unsound vessels o'er again,

For sail they cannot; and instead thereof
One makes his vessel new, and one recaulks
The ribs of that which many a voyage has made;

One hammers at the prow, one at the stern,
This one makes oars, and that one cordage twists,

Another mends the mainsail and the mizzen;

Thus, not by fire, but by the art divine,
Was boiling down below there a dense pitch
Which upon every side the bank belimed.

I saw it, but I did not see within it
Aught but the bubbles that the boiling raised,
And all swell up and resubside compressed.

The while below there fixedly I gazed,
My Leader, crying out: "Beware, beware!"
Drew me unto himself from where I stood.

Then I turned round, as one who is impatient
To see what it behoves him to escape,
And whom a sudden terror doth unman,

Who, while he looks, delays not his departure;
And I beheld behind us a black devil,
Running along upon the crag, approach.

Ah, how ferocious was he in his aspect!

From bridge to bridge talking of other things
I do not wish to include in my Comedy,
We came along to the summit when

We halted to look at another fissure
Of Malebolge and other vain laments;
I thought it was terribly dark.

As in the Arsenal of the Venetians,
Tenacious pitch boils in the winter
To be smeared around unsound vessels,

For they cannot sail; Instead
One made a new vessel and one recaulked
The ribs of the vessel that made many voyages;

One hammered at the prow, one at the stern,
This one made oars while another twisted the ropes,
And another mended the mainsail and the mizzen;

Thus, not by fire, but by the divine art,
A dense pitch was boiling down below there
Bubbling along every bank.

I saw it, but couldn't see in it
Except for the bubbles being raised,
Swelling, bursting, and resubmitting.

While I fixed my gaze below,
My leader cried out: "Beware, beware!"
Drawing me into himself, from where I stood.

Then I turned around impatiently
To see what I had just escaped
And what had scared him like one,

Who looks back while leaving;
And I saw a black devil behind us,
Running along the crag, approaching us.

Ah, how ferocious he was!

And how he seemed to me in action ruthless,
With open wings and light upon his feet!

His shoulders, which sharp-pointed were and high,
A sinner did encumber with both haunches,
And he held clutched the sinews of the feet.

From off our bridge, he said: "O Malebranche,
Behold one of the elders of Saint Zita;
Plunge him beneath, for I return for others

Unto that town, which is well furnished with them.
All there are barrators, except Bonturo;
No into Yes for money there is changed."

He hurled him down, and over the hard crag
Turned round, and never was a mastiff loosened

In so much hurry to pursue a thief.

The other sank, and rose again face downward;
But the demons, under cover of the bridge,
Cried: "Here the Santo Volto has no place!

Here swims one otherwise than in the Serchio;
Therefore, if for our gaffs thou wishest not,
Do not uplift thyself above the pitch."

They seized him then with more than a hundred rakes;

They said: "It here behoves thee to dance covered,
That, if thou canst, thou secretly mayest pilfer."

Not otherwise the cooks their scullions make
Immerse into the middle of the caldron
The meat with hooks, so that it may not float.

Said the good Master to me: "That it be not

Apparent thou art here, crouch thyself down
Behind a jag, that thou mayest have some screen;

And for no outrage that is done to me
Be thou afraid, because these things I know,
For once before was I in such a scuffle."

Then he passed on beyond the bridge's head,
And as upon the sixth bank he arrived,

And how he seemed to me in ruthless action,
With open wings and light feet!

His sharp-pointed shoulders, were high,
He carried a sinner on both haunches
Clutching the sinews of the feet.

From off our bridge, he said: "Oh Malebranche,
Behold one of the elders of Saint Zita,
Plunge him below, for I must return for others

In the town, which is well furnished with them.
All of these are cheaters, except Bonturo;
They turn nos into yeses in exchange for money."

He hurled him down over the hard crag
Turned around and there never was a loosened
mastiff
In such a hurry to pursue a thief.

The other sank and rose again;
But the demons, under the bridge,
Cried: "Here the Santo Voto has no place!

Here one does not swim in the Serchio;
Therefore, if you do not wish for our prongs,
Do not lift yourself up above the pitch."

They seized him then with more than a hundred
pitchforks;
Saying: "It is better here to dance under cover,
So if you can, you may pilfer secretly."

They looked like cooks, who make servants
Immerse, into the middle of the caldron,
Meat with hooks, so it may not float up.

The good Master said to me: "So they won't see
you,
Crouch down behind the jagged rock
And hide yourself;

Do not fear any outrage done to me,
Because I know how these things work,
Having been in such a scuffle, before."

Then he passed on beyond the head of the bridge,
And when he arrived upon the sixth bank,

Need was for him to have a steadfast front.	*He needed a steadfast front.*
With the same fury, and the same uproar, As dogs leap out upon a mendicant, Who on a sudden begs, where'er he stops,	*With the same fury and uproar,* *As dogs leap out upon a beggar,* *Who begs wherever he stops,*
They issued from beneath the little bridge, And turned against him all their grappling-irons; But he cried out: "Be none of you malignant!	*They came from underneath the little bridge,* *And turned their grappling irons against him;* *But he cried out: "Do not be distressed!*
Before those hooks of yours lay hold of me, Let one of you step forward, who may hear me, And then take counsel as to grappling me."	*Before those hooks of yours lay hold of me,* *Let one of you come forward and listen to me,* *Then reconsider fighting me."*
They all cried out: "Let Malacoda go;" Whereat one started, and the rest stood still, And he came to him, saying: "What avails it?"	*They all cried out: "Let Malacoda go;"* *Whereupon one started, and the rest stood still,* *And he came saying: "What are you doing here?"*
"Thinkest thou, Malacoda, to behold me Advanced into this place," my Master said, "Safe hitherto from all your skill of fence,	*"Think, Malacoda, to see me* *Here in this place," my Master said,* *"Would I be safe from the defenses in place,*
Without the will divine, and fate auspicious? Let me go on, for it in Heaven is willed That I another show this savage road."	*If it were not for divine will and auspicious fate?* *Let me go on, for it is willed in Heaven* *That I show someone this savage road."*
Then was his arrogance so humbled in him, That he let fall his grapnel at his feet, And to the others said: "Now strike him not."	*He was so humbled,* *That he let his grapnel fall at his feet* *And said to the others: "Do not strike him now."*
And unto me my Guide: "O thou, who sittest Among the splinters of the bridge crouched down, Securely now return to me again."	*My Guide continued to me: "You, who sits* *Crouched down among the splinters of the bridge,* *May return safely to me again."*
Wherefore I started and came swiftly to him; And all the devils forward thrust themselves, So that I feared they would not keep their compact.	*So I came swiftly to him;* *And all the devils thrust themselves forward,* *So that I feared they would not keep their compact.*
And thus beheld I once afraid the soldiers Who issued under safeguard from Caprona, Seeing themselves among so many foes.	*Thus, I became like the scared soldiers* *Issued under safeguard from Caprona,* *Who saw themselves among so many foes.*
Close did I press myself with all my person Beside my Leader, and turned not mine eyes From off their countenance, which was not good.	*I pressed closer to my Leader,* *And did not move my eyes* *From theirs, which was not good.*
They lowered their rakes, and "Wilt thou have me hit him,"	*They lowered their rakes, and "Do you* *want me to hit him,"*

They said to one another, "on the rump?"
And answered: "Yes; see that thou nick him with it."

But the same demon who was holding parley
With my Conductor turned him very quickly,
And said: "Be quiet, be quiet, Scarmiglione

Then said to us: "You can no farther go
Forward upon this crag, because is lying
All shattered, at the bottom, the sixth arch.

And if it still doth please you to go onward,
Pursue your way along upon this rock;
Near is another crag that yields a path.

Yesterday, five hours later than this hour,
One thousand and two hundred sixty-six
Years were complete, that here the way was broken.

I send in that direction some of mine
To see if any one doth air himself;
Go ye with them; for they will not be vicious.

Step forward, Alichino and Calcabrina,"
Began he to cry out, "and thou, Cagnazzo;
And Barbariccia, do thou guide the ten

Come forward, Libicocco and Draghignazzo,
And tusked Ciriatto and Graffiacane,
And Farfarello and mad Rubicante

Search ye all round about the boiling pitch;
Let these be safe as far as the next crag,
That all unbroken passes o'er the dens."

"O me! what is it, Master, that I see?
Pray let us go," I said, "without an escort,
If thou knowest how, since for myself I ask none.

If thou art as observant as thy wont is,
Dost thou not see that they do gnash their teeth,
And with their brows are threatening woe to us?"

And he to me: "I will not have thee fear;
Let them gnash on, according to their fancy,
Because they do it for those boiling wretches."

Along the left-hand dike they wheeled about;

They said to one another, "on the rump?"
And some answered: "Yes; see that you nick him
with it."
But the same demon who was negotiating
With my Conductor, turned to them very quickly,
And said: "Be quiet, be quiet, Scarmiglione,"

Then he said to us: "You can go no farther
Upon this crag, because it is lying
Shattered, at the bottom of the sixth arch.

And if it pleases you to go onward,
Take this way along this rock;
There is another path.

Yesterday, five hours before now,
And one thousand and two hundred sixty-six
Years ago, the way was broken.

I will send some of mine in that direction
To see if anyone is ahead;
Go with them, for they will not be vicious.

Step forward, Alichino and Calcabrina,"
He began, "and you, Cagnazzo,
And Barbariccia, guide the ten.

Come forward, Libicocco and Draghignazzo,
And tusked Ciriatto and Graffiacane,
And Farfarello and mad Rubicante;

Search all around the boiling pitch;
Let these be safe as far as the next crag
That passes unbroken over the dens."

"Oh me! What is it, Master, that I see?
Please let us go," I said, "without an escort,
As you know, I do not ask for one myself.

If you are very observant,
Don't you see that they gnash their teeth,
And threaten us with their brows?"

He replied: "I will not have you fear;
Let them gnash on as they wish,
Because they do it for those boiling wretches."

Along the left side of the dike, they wheeled about;

But first had each one thrust his tongue between
His teeth towards their leader for a signal;

And he had made a trumpet of his rump.

But first, each one thrust out his tongue between
His teeth towards their leader as a signal;

And he made a trumpet from his rump.

Inferno: Canto XXII

I have erewhile seen horsemen moving camp,
Begin the storming, and their muster make,
And sometimes starting off for their escape;

I have seen horseman moving camp before,
Storming about and gathering their muster
Before starting their escape;

Vaunt-couriers have I seen upon your land,
O Aretines, and foragers go forth,
Tournaments stricken, and the joustings run,

I have seen Vaunt-couriers upon land,
Oh Aretines, and foragers going forth,
To tournaments and jousting,

Sometimes with trumpets and sometimes with bells,
With kettle-drums, and signals of the castles,
And with our own, and with outlandish things,

Sometimes with trumpets and bells,
With kettle-drums, and signals of their castles.
I have seen many outlandish things.

But never yet with bagpipe so uncouth

But I have never seen or heard anything so
uncouth,

Did I see horsemen move, nor infantry,
Nor ship by any sign of land or star.

Among horsemen or infantry,
By ship, or land, or star.

We went upon our way with the ten demons;
Ah, savage company! but in the church
With saints, and in the tavern with the gluttons!

We went upon our way with the ten demons;
Ah, what savage company! Only in the church
With saints, and in the tavern with gluttons!

Ever upon the pitch was my intent,
To see the whole condition of that Bolgia,
And of the people who therein were burned.

I was intent on seeing the pitch,
The whole condition of that Bolgia,
And of the people who were burning within.

Even as the dolphins, when they make a sign
To mariners by arching of the back,
That they should counsel take to save their vessel,

Even as the dolphins, who signal mariners
By arching their backs,
So they should take counsel to save their vessel,

Thus sometimes, to alleviate his pain,
One of the sinners would display his back,
And in less time conceal it than it lightens.

One of the sinners, to alleviate the pain,
Would display his back,
Only to conceal it again before it lightened.

As on the brink of water in a ditch
The frogs stand only with their muzzles out,
So that they hide their feet and other bulk,

Like frogs on the brink of a watery ditch
Standing with only their muzzles out,
So that their bodies and feet are hidden,

So upon every side the sinners stood;
But ever as Barbariccia near them came,
Thus underneath the boiling they withdrew.

The sinners stood upon every side;
But just as Barbariccia came near them,
They withdrew underneath the boiling water.

I saw, and still my heart doth shudder at it,

I saw and my heart still shudders to remember,

One waiting thus, even as it comes to pass
One frog remains, and down another dives;

And Graffiacan, who most confronted him,
Grappled him by his tresses smeared with pitch,

And drew him up, so that he seemed an otter.

I knew, before, the names of all of them,
So had I noted them when they were chosen,
And when they called each other, listened how.

"O Rubicante, see that thou do lay
Thy claws upon him, so that thou mayst flay him,"
Cried all together the accursed ones.

And I: "My Master, see to it, if thou canst,
That thou mayst know who is the luckless wight,
Thus come into his adversaries' hands."

Near to the side of him my Leader drew,
Asked of him whence he was; and he replied:
"I in the kingdom of Navarre was born;

My mother placed me servant to a lord,
For she had borne me to a ribald knave,
Destroyer of himself and of his things.

Then I domestic was of good King Thibault;
I set me there to practise barratry,
For which I pay the reckoning in this heat."

And Ciriatto, from whose mouth projected,
On either side, a tusk, as in a boar,
Caused him to feel how one of them could rip.

Among malicious cats the mouse had come;
But Barbariccia clasped him in his arms,
And said: "Stand ye aside, while I enfork him."

And to my Master he turned round his head;
"Ask him again," he said, "if more thou wish
To know from him, before some one destroy him."

The Guide: "Now tell then of the other culprits;

Knowest thou any one who is a Latian,

One waiting, like a frog that remains
While another dives down;

And Graffiacan, confronted him,
Grappling him by his tresses, smeared him with pitch,
And drew him up, so that he seemed like an otter.

Before I knew the names of them all,
I had noted them when they were chosen,
And when and how they called to each other.

"Oh Rubicante, see that you do lay
Your claws in him, so that you may flay him,"
The cursed ones cried altogether.

And I responded: "My Master, see if you can
Find out who the luckless soul is
That comes into his adversaries' hands."

My Leader drew nearer to his side,
And asked him who he was;
He replied: "I was born in the kingdom of Navarre;

My mother placed me as a servant to a lord,
For she had lain with a ribald knave,
Who destroyed himself and his things.

Then I worked for the good King Thibault;
There I began to steal,
For which I pay the reckoning in this heat."

Ciriatto, who had tusks, like a boar,
On either side of his mouth,
Made him feel how one of them could rip.

The mouse had come among the malicious cats;
Barbariccia clasped him in his arms,
And said: "Stand aside, while I fork him."

Then he said to my Master;
"Ask him again, if he wants to know more
From him, before someone destroys him."

The Guide: "Tell us of the other culprits under the pitch
You know who are Latin.

Under the pitch?" And he: "I separated

Lately from one who was a neighbour to it;
Would that I still were covered up with him,
For I should fear not either claw nor hook!"

And Libicocco: "We have borne too much;"
And with his grapnel seized him by the arm,
So that, by rending, he tore off a tendon.

Eke Draghignazzo wished to pounce upon him
Down at the legs; whence their Decurion
Turned round and round about with evil look.

When they again somewhat were pacified,
Of him, who still was looking at his wound,
Demanded my Conductor without stay:

"Who was that one, from whom a luckless parting
Thou sayest thou hast made, to come ashore?"
And he replied: "It was the Friar Gomita,

He of Gallura, vessel of all fraud,
Who had the enemies of his Lord in hand,
And dealt so with them each exults thereat;

Money he took, and let them smoothly off,
As he says; and in other offices
A barrator was he, not mean but sovereign.

Foregathers with him one Don Michael Zanche
Of Logodoro; and of Sardinia
To gossip never do their tongues feel tired.

O me! see that one, how he grinds his teeth;
Still farther would I speak, but am afraid
Lest he to scratch my itch be making ready."

And the grand Provost, turned to Farfarello,
Who rolled his eyes about as if to strike,
Said: "Stand aside there, thou malicious bird."

"If you desire either to see or hear,"
The terror-stricken recommenced thereon,
"Tuscans or Lombards, I will make them come.

But let the Malebranche cease a little,
So that these may not their revenges fear,

And he returned: "I just separated

From one who was a neighbor to it;
I wish I were still covered up with him,
Then I wouldn't fear the claw or the hook!"

Then Libicocco: "We have allowed enough;"
And with his grapnel seized him by the arm,
So it tore off a tendon.

Draghignazzo wished to pounce upon him
Down at the legs, when Decurion
Turned around with an evil look.

When they were pacified,
While looking at his wound,
My Conductor demanded without hesitating:

"Who was the one you parted from
When you came ashore?"
And he replied: "It was the Friar Gomita,

Of Gallura, a vessel of all fraud,
Who had the enemies of his Lord in hand,
Where he dealt with them by extortion;

And by taking money, let them off smoothly,
As he says; and in other offices
He was a thief, but he was sovereign.

If you put him with Don Michael Zanche
Of Logodoro and Sardinia
Whose tongues never get tired of gossiping.

Oh me! See how that one grinds his teeth;
I would speak more, but I am afraid
That he is getting ready to scratch me like an itch."
And the grand Provost, turned to Farfarello,
Who rolled his eyes around as if to strike,
Saying: "Stand aside there, you malicious bird."

"If you desire to see or hear,"
The terror-stricken soul continued,
"I will make the Tuscans or Lombards come.

But let the Malebranche stop a little,
So they will not fear their vengeance,

And I, down sitting in this very place,

For one that I am will make seven come,
When I shall whistle, as our custom is
To do whenever one of us comes out."

Cagnazzo at these words his muzzle lifted,

Shaking his head, and said: "Just hear the trick
Which he has thought of, down to throw himself!"

Whence he, who snares in great abundance had,
Responded: "I by far too cunning am,
When I procure for mine a greater sadness."

Alichin held not in, but running counter
Unto the rest, said to him: "If thou dive,
I will not follow thee upon the gallop,

But I will beat my wings above the pitch;
The height be left, and be the bank a shield
To see if thou alone dost countervail us."

O thou who readest, thou shalt hear new sport!
Each to the other side his eyes averted;
He first, who most reluctant was to do it.

The Navarrese selected well his time;
Planted his feet on land, and in a moment
Leaped, and released himself from their design.

Whereat each one was suddenly stung with shame,

But he most who was cause of the defeat;
Therefore he moved, and cried: "Thou art o'ertakern."

But little it availed, for wings could not
Outstrip the fear; the other one went under,
And, flying, upward he his breast directed;

Not otherwise the duck upon a sudden
Dives under, when the falcon is approaching,
And upward he returneth cross and weary.

Infuriate at the mockery, Calcabrina
Flying behind him followed close, desirous

And while I sit here in this very place,

Being who I am, will make seven come,
When I whistle as is our custom
Whenever one of us comes out."

At these words Cagnazzo lifted his muzzle,

And shaking his head, said: "Just hear the trick
Which he has thought of to throw himself down!"

When the one who snared so much
Responded: "I am by far too cunning,
When I delegate sadness."

Suddenly Alichin came running
And to the rest said: "If you dive,
I will not follow you running,

But I will beat my wings above the pitch;
Nothing will be left but the bank
To see if you evaded us."

Oh reader, you should have heard this new sport!
Each averted his eyes to the other;
First, the one who was most reluctant to do it.

The Navarrese selected his time well;
He planted his feet on land and in a moment
Leapt and freed himself from their plan.

Whereupon each one was suddenly stung with
shame,
But most by the one who caused the defeat;
Therefore he moved, and cried: "You are
overthrown."

But his wings could not
Outfly the fear, and the other one went under,
Flying upwards with his breast directed,

Like a duck during a sudden
Dive, when the falcon is approaching,
Who returns upwards cross and weary.

Infuriated by such mockery, Calcabrina
Flying behind him followed closely in hopes

The other should escape, to have a quarrel.

And when the barrator had disappeared,
He turned his talons upon his companion,
And grappled with him right above the moat.

But sooth the other was a doughty sparhawk
To clapperclaw him well; and both of them
Fell in the middle of the boiling pond.

A sudden intercessor was the heat;
But ne'ertheless of rising there was naught,
To such degree they had their wings belimed.

Lamenting with the others, Barbariccia
Made four of them fly to the other side
With all their gaffs, and very speedily

This side and that they to their posts descended;
They stretched their hooks towards the pitch-ensnared,

Who were already baked within the crust,

And in this manner busied did we leave them.

*The other should escape giving him means to have
a quarrel.
When the thief disappeared,
He turned his talons upon his companion,
And grappled with him right above the moat.*

*However the other was a brave hawk
To claw him well; and both of them
Fell in the middle of the boiling pond.*

*The heat was a sudden intercessor;
But there was no rising up
For they had burnt their wings.*

*Lamenting with the others, Barbariccia
Made four of them fly quickly to the other side
With all of their gaffs.*

*On my side, the rest descended to their posts;
They stretched their hooks towards the victims of
the pitch,
Who were already baked within the crust,*

So we left them.

Inferno: Canto XXIII

Silent, alone, and without company
We went, the one in front, the other after,

As go the Minor Friars along their way.

Upon the fable of Aesop was directed
My thought, by reason of the present quarrel,
Where he has spoken of the frog and mouse;

For 'mo' and 'issa' are not more alike
Than this one is to that, if well we couple
End and beginning with a steadfast mind.

And even as one thought from another springs,
So afterward from that was born another,
Which the first fear within me double made.

Thus did I ponder: "These on our account
Are laughed to scorn, with injury and scoff
So great, that much I think it must annoy them.

If anger be engrafted on ill-will,
They will come after us more merciless
Than dog upon the leveret which he seizes,"

I felt my hair stand all on end already
With terror, and stood backwardly intent,
When said I: "Master, if thou hidest not

Thyself and me forthwith, of Malebranche
I am in dread; we have them now behind us;
I so imagine them, I already feel them."

And he: "If I were made of leaded glass,
Thine outward image I should not attract
Sooner to me than I imprint the inner.

Just now thy thoughts came in among my own,
With similar attitude and similar face,
So that of both one counsel sole I made.

If peradventure the right bank so slope

Silent, alone, and without company,
We went with the Master in front and me
following,
Like the Minor Friars along their way.

I thought about the fable of Aesop
Reminded by the present quarrel,
Where he spoke of the frog and mouse;

For 'mo' and 'issa' are not more alike
Than this one is to that, if we compare
The end to the beginning with a steadfast mind.

And as one thought leads to another,
I had a feeling
Which made me double over with fear.

I thought: "Because of us, those demons
Are being laughed at and scorned with injury,
So great, that they may become annoyed with us.

If anger be the predecessor to ill-will,
They will purse us mercilessly,
Like a dog after a rabbit."

I felt my hair stand on end
And with terror, stood looking backwards,
Saying: "Master, if you do not

Hide us right now,
I fear the Malebranche may be behind us;
It's like I can feel them."

And he replied: "If you were made of glass,
Your outward image would be
More revealing than your inner thoughts I heard.

Just now your thoughts came to me,
And in addition to your attitude and face,
I figured out what was wrong.

If, by chance, the right bank slopes

That we to the next Bolgia can descend,
We shall escape from the imagined chase."

Not yet he finished rendering such opinion,
When I beheld them come with outstretched wings,

Not far remote, with will to seize upon us.

My Leader on a sudden seized me up,
Even as a mother who by noise is wakened,
And close beside her sees the enkindled flames,

Who takes her son, and flies, and does not stop,
Having more care of him than of herself,
So that she clothes her only with a shift;

And downward from the top of the hard bank
Supine he gave him to the pendent rock,
That one side of the other Bolgia walls.

Ne'er ran so swiftly water through a sluice
To turn the wheel of any land-built mill,
When nearest to the paddles it approaches,

As did my Master down along that border,
Bearing me with him on his breast away,
As his own son, and not as a companion.

Hardly the bed of the ravine below
His feet had reached, ere they had reached the hill
Right over us; but he was not afraid;

For the high Providence, which had ordained
To place them ministers of the fifth moat,
The power of thence departing took from all.

A painted people there below we found,
Who went about with footsteps very slow,
Weeping and in their semblance tired and vanquished.

They had on mantles with the hoods low down
Before their eyes, and fashioned of the cut
That in Cologne they for the monks are made.

Without, they gilded are so that it dazzles;
But inwardly all leaden and so heavy
That Frederick used to put them on of straw.

So we can descend to the next Bolgia,
We can escape from your imagined chase."

He had not yet finished rendering his opinion,
When I saw them coming nearer with outstretched wings,
In order to seize us.

Suddenly, my Leader seized me up,
Like a mother awakened by a noise,
Who sees a fire burning beside her,

And takes her son, fleeing without stopping,
Caring more for him than herself,
So that she barely dresses;

Downward from the top of the hard bank,
He threw himself on the jutted rock,
Adjacent to the other Bolgia walls.

Water never ran so swiftly through a channel,
To turn the wheel of a mill,
When the nearest paddle approaches,

As my Master did along that border,
Carrying me with him on his breast,
Like a son, not a companion.

He had hardly reached the bed of the ravine below
Before they had reached the hill
Right over us; but he was not afraid;

For the high Providence, who had ordained
The demons ministers of the fifth moat,
Took the power of departure from them all.

We found below a painted people,
Who went about with very slow footsteps,
Weeping, with tired and vanquished countenances.

They had on mantles with low hoods down
Over their eyes, with haircuts resembling
The monks of Cologne.

On the outside they dazzled;
But inwardly the cloaks were heavy and lead-filled
Like Frederick used to put on straw.

O everlastingly fatiguing mantle!
Again we turned us, still to the left hand
Along with them, intent on their sad plaint;

But owing to the weight, that weary folk
Came on so tardily, that we were new
In company at each motion of the haunch.

Whence I unto my Leader: "See thou find
Some one who may by deed or name be known,
And thus in going move thine eye about."

And one, who understood the Tuscan speech,
Cried to us from behind: "Stay ye your feet,
Ye, who so run athwart the dusky air!

Perhaps thou'lt have from me what thou demandest."

Whereat the Leader turned him, and said: "Wait,
And then according to his pace proceed."

I stopped, and two beheld I show great haste
Of spirit, in their faces, to be with me;
But the burden and the narrow way delayed them.

When they came up, long with an eye askance
They scanned me without uttering a word.
Then to each other turned, and said together:

"He by the action of his throat seems living;
And if they dead are, by what privilege
Go they uncovered by the heavy stole?"

Then said to me: "Tuscan, who to the college
Of miserable hypocrites art come,
Do not disdain to tell us who thou art."

And I to them: "Born was I, and grew up
In the great town on the fair river of Arno,
And with the body am I've always had.

But who are ye, in whom there trickles down
Along your cheeks such grief as I behold?
And what pain is upon you, that so sparkles?"

And one replied to me: "These orange cloaks
Are made of lead so heavy, that the weights
Cause in this way their balances to creak.

Oh everlasting and tiring mantle!
Again we turned to the left
And walked along with them on their sad march.

Due to the weight, the weary folk
Trudged along so slowly
That we were in new company at each leg of the way.
When I said to my Leader: "See if you can find
Someone, whom I might know by deed or name,
While we move about."

And one, recognizing my Tuscan accent,
Cried to us from behind: "Stop moving,
You, who are running in the dusky air!

Perhaps I can fill the requirements which you asked."
The Leader turned to him and said: "Wait,
Let's walk with him at his pace."

I stopped and saw two spirits
With great haste in their faces to be with me;
But the burden and the narrow way delayed them.

When they caught up,
They looked at me without uttering a word.
Then they turned to each other and said:

"He seems to be living by looking at his throat;
And if they are dead, by what privilege
Do they go uncovered by the heavy coat?"

To me they said: "Tuscan, who visits
The college of miserable hypocrites,
Do not hesitate to tell us who you are."

I replied: "I was born and grew up
In the great town on the fair river, Arno,
And I've always had this body.

But who are you, who has trickling down
Upon your cheeks such grief?
And what is so sparkling that causes you pain?"

One said to me: "These orange cloaks
Are made of lead so heavy that the weights
Cause their balances to creak.

Frati Gaudenti were we, and Bolognese;
I Catalano, and he Loderingo
Named, and together taken by thy city,

As the wont is to take one man alone,
For maintenance of its peace; and we were such
That still it is apparent round Gardingo."

"O Friars," began I, "your iniquitous. . ."
But said no more; for to mine eyes there rushed
One crucified with three stakes on the ground.

When me he saw, he writhed himself all over,
Blowing into his beard with suspirations;
And the Friar Catalan, who noticed this,

Said to me: "This transfixed one, whom thou seest,
Counselled the Pharisees that it was meet
To put one man to torture for the people.

Crosswise and naked is he on the path,
As thou perceivest; and he needs must feel,
Whoever passes, first how much he weighs;

And in like mode his father-in-law is punished
Within this moat, and the others of the council,

Which for the Jews was a malignant seed."

And thereupon I saw Virgilius marvel
O'er him who was extended on the cross
So vilely in eternal banishment.

Then he directed to the Friar this voice:
"Be not displeased, if granted thee, to tell us

If to the right hand any pass slope down

By which we two may issue forth from here,
Without constraining some of the black angels
To come and extricate us from this deep."

Then he made answer: "Nearer than thou hopest
There is a rock, that forth from the great circle
Proceeds, and crosses all the cruel valleys,

We were Frati Gaudenti from Bolognese;
I am Catalano and he is Loderingo.
We were taken by your city,

As the custom is to take one man alone,
To maintain peace; and we were such
That is still apparent around Gardingo."

"Oh Friars," I began, "your iniquitous..."
But I said no more, because before my eyes
I saw a man crucified with three stakes on the
ground.
When he saw me, he writhed all over,
Blowing into his beard great sighs;
And the Friar Catalan, who noticed this,

Said to me: "This transfixed one you see was
The counselor of the Pharisees,
Who put one man to torture for all of mankind.

He lies crosswise and naked on the path,
As you can see; and he must feel
The weight of whoever passes over him;

Similarly, his father-in-law is punished
Within this moat, as well as the others in the
council,
Which was a malignant seed for the Jews."

Then I saw Virgil marveling
Over the man extended on the cross,
So vilely punished in eternal banishment.

He directed his voice to the Friar:
"Please do not be offended, if we ask you to tell
us,
If there is a slope on the right,

By which we may leave from here,
Without running into some of the black angels
Who may want to extricate us from this deep."

He answered: "Nearer than you hope,
There is a rock that proceeds from the great circle
And crosses all the cruel valleys,

Save that at this 'tis broken, and does not bridge it;

You will be able to mount up the ruin,
That sidelong slopes and at the bottom rises."

The Leader stood awhile with head bowed down;

Then said: "The business badly he recounted
Who grapples with his hook the sinners yonder."

And the Friar: "Many of the Devil's vices
Once heard I at Bologna, and among them,
That he's a liar and the father of lies."

Thereat my Leader with great strides went on,
Somewhat disturbed with anger in his looks;
Whence from the heavy-laden I departed

After the prints of his beloved feet.

But the other way is broken and does not permit access;
You will be able to climb up the ruin,
That slopes along the side and rises at the bottom."
The Leader stood awhile with his head bowed down;
Then he said: "He remembers the bad business
Of those who grapple sinners with his hook."

And the Friar: "Among many of the Devil's vices,
I heard once at Bologna, is
He is a liar, the father of lies."

Then my Leader with great strides went on,
Looking somewhat disturbed,
Where I departed from the heavy-laden

Following the beloved's footprints.

Inferno: Canto XXIV

In that part of the youthful year wherein
The Sun his locks beneath Aquarius tempers,
And now the nights draw near to half the day,

What time the hoar-frost copies on the ground
The outward semblance of her sister white,
But little lasts the temper of her pen,

The husbandman, whose forage faileth him,
Rises, and looks, and seeth the champaign
All gleaming white, whereat he beats his flank,

Returns in doors, and up and down laments,
Like a poor wretch, who knows not what to do;
Then he returns and hope revives again,

Seeing the world has changed its countenance
In little time, and takes his shepherd's crook,
And forth the little lambs to pasture drives.

Thus did the Master fill me with alarm,
When I beheld his forehead so disturbed,
And to the ailment came as soon the plaster.

For as we came unto the ruined bridge,
The Leader turned to me with that sweet look
Which at the mountain's foot I first beheld.

His arms he opened, after some advisement
Within himself elected, looking first
Well at the ruin, and laid hold of me.

And even as he who acts and meditates,
For aye it seems that he provides beforehand,
So upward lifting me towards the summit

Of a huge rock, he scanned another crag,
Saying: "To that one grapple afterwards,
But try first if 'tis such that it will hold thee."

This was no way for one clothed with a cloak;
For hardly we, he light, and I pushed upward,

In the year when,
The Sun, locked beneath Aquarius, tempered
So the nights drew to half the day,

The frost whitened the ground,
Revealing the time,
But this was not everlasting.

The shepherd, who failed at foraging,
Arose and looked, seeing the
Gleaming white, whereupon he beat himself

And returned indoors to lament
Like a poor wretch, who doesn't know what to do;
Then, returning with renewed hope,

He saw the world had changed again,
And in no time, took his staff,
And drove the little lambs to pasture.

Thus, my Master filled me with alarm,
When I saw the stress on his forehead
Then I saw what bothered him,

For we came to the ruined bridge, and
The Leader turned to me with that sweet look
When I first saw the foot of the mountain

He opened his arms, after thinking
To himself and looking well at the first ruin
He took hold of me.

And like one who acts and after meditating
For yes, it seemed like he had plan,
He lifted me upwards toward the summit

Of a huge rock, while scanning another,
Saying: "Try that one next,
But make sure it will hold you."

This was no way for one with a cloak;
For we hardly were able to climb

Were able to ascend from jag to jag.

And had it not been, that upon that precinct
Shorter was the ascent than on the other,
He I know not, but I had been dead beat.

But because Malebolge tow'rds the mouth
Of the profoundest well is all inclining,
The structure of each valley doth import

That one bank rises and the other sinks.
Still we arrived at length upon the point
Wherefrom the last stone breaks itself asunder.

The breath was from my lungs so milked away,
When I was up, that I could go no farther,
Nay, I sat down upon my first arrival.

"Now it behoves thee thus to put off sloth,"
My Master said; "for sitting upon down,
Or under quilt, one cometh not to fame

Withouten which whoso his life consumes
Such vestige leaveth of himself on earth,
As smoke in air or in the water foam.

And therefore raise thee up, o'ercome the anguish
With spirit that o'ercometh every battle,
If with its heavy body it sink not.

A longer stairway it behoves thee mount;
'Tis not enough from these to have departed;
Let it avail thee, if thou understand me."

Then I uprose, showing myself provided
Better with breath than I did feel myself,
And said: "Go on, for I am strong and bold."

Upward we took our way along the crag,
Which jagged was, and narrow, and difficult,
And more precipitous far than that before.

Speaking I went, not to appear exhausted;

Whereat a voice from the next moat came forth,
Not well adapted to articulate words.

With him being so light and me pulling up.

And had it not been, that that area
Was shorter than the other,
I don't know about him, but I would be dead.

But because of the Malebolge, towards the mouth
Of the profoundest well, everything was inclining
With the structure of the valley being

While one bank rises, the other sinks.
Still, we arrived after some time at the point
Where from the last stone it broke.

My breath was so shallow,
When I ascended, that I could not go any farther,
So, I sat down once we arrived.

"Now it would do you well to not be lazy,"
My Master said, "for sitting down,
Or resting, keeps one from achieving their goals,

Without which his life becomes
Unremarkable, leaving him like
Smoke in the air or water in the foam.

Therefore, get up and overcome the anguish
With a spirit that has overcome everything else,
And doesn't let the body collapse.

It will serve you to mount a longer stairway;
It's not enough to have climbed thus far;
If you understand me, get up."

Then I arose, showing I had
Regained my breath, better than I really had,
And said: "Go on, for I am strong and bold."

We took our way along the crag,
Which was jagged, narrow, and difficult,
And more precipitous than before.

I went along without speaking to not appear
exhausted;
When a voice from the next moat came forth,
Speaking inarticulately.

I know not what it said, though o'er the back	*I did not know what it said, though I was over the back*
I now was of the arch that passes there; But he seemed moved to anger who was speaking.	*Of the arch that passed there; But he seemed very angry.*
I was bent downward, but my living eyes	*I was bent downward, but with my living eyes*
Could not attain the bottom, for the dark; Wherefore I: "Master, see that thou arrive	*I could not see the bottom, because of the dark; Therefore, I said: "Master, let's go to*
At the next round, and let us descend the wall; For as from hence I hear and understand not, So I look down and nothing I distinguish."	*The next round and descend the wall; Because I cannot hear or understand, Nor can I see anything when I look down."*
"Other response," he said, "I make thee not, Except the doing; for the modest asking Ought to be followed by the deed in silence."	*"I cannot give you answer," he said, "Except show you the way; for asking modestly One should proceed silently in completing the deed."*
We from the bridge descended at its head, Where it connects itself with the eighth bank, And then was manifest to me the Bolgia;	*We descended then from the bridge, Where it connected itself with the eighth bank, And then I saw the Bolgia;*
And I beheld therein a terrible throng Of serpents, and of such a monstrous kind, That the remembrance still congeals my blood	*Within, I saw a terrible throng Of serpents, and of such a monstrous variety, That the memory still congeals my blood.*
Let Libya boast no longer with her sand; For if Chelydri, Jaculi, and Phareae She breeds, with Cenchri and with Amphisbaena,	*Let Libya boast no longer with her sand; For if Chelydri, Jaculi, and Pharae Breeds with Cenchri and Amphisbaena,*
Neither so many plagues nor so malignant	*Neither could produce as many plagues so malignant*
E'er showed she with all Ethiopia, Nor with whatever on the Red Sea is!	*In all of Ethiopia either, Or where the Red Sea is!*
Among this cruel and most dismal throng People were running naked and affrighted. Without the hope of hole or heliotrope.	*Among this cruel and dismal group, People were running naked and frightened, Without the hope of a hole or plant.*
They had their hands with serpents bound behind them;	*They had their hands bound behind them with serpents;*
These riveted upon their reins the tail And head, and were in front of them entwined.	*Their tails and heads writhing And winding around in front of them.*
And lo! at one who was upon our side There darted forth a serpent, which transfixed him There where the neck is knotted to the shoulders.	*And Lord! One who was by our side Was transfixed by a serpent darting forth And biting him around the neck.*

Nor 'O' so quickly e'er, nor 'I' was written,
As he took fire, and burned; and ashes wholly
Behoved it that in falling he became.

And when he on the ground was thus destroyed,
The ashes drew together, and of themselves
Into himself they instantly returned.

Even thus by the great sages 'tis confessed
The phoenix dies, and then is born again,
When it approaches its five-hundredth year;

On herb or grain it feeds not in its life,
But only on tears of incense and amomum,
And nard and myrrh are its last winding-sheet.

And as he is who falls, and knows not how,
By force of demons who to earth down drag him,

Or other oppilation that binds man,

When he arises and around him looks,
Wholly bewildered by the mighty anguish
Which he has suffered, and in looking sighs;

Such was that sinner after he had risen.
Justice of God! O how severe it is,
That blows like these in vengeance poureth down!

The Guide thereafter asked him who he was;
Whence he replied: "I rained from Tuscany
A short time since into this cruel gorge.

A bestial life, and not a human, pleased me,
Even as the mule I was; I'm Vanni Fucci,
Beast, and Pistoia was my worthy den."

And I unto the Guide: "Tell him to stir not,
And ask what crime has thrust him here below,

For once a man of blood and wrath I saw him."

And the sinner, who had heard, dissembled not,
But unto me directed mind and face,
And with a melancholy shame was painted.

Then said: "It pains me more that thou hast caught me

No letter has ever been written as quickly,
As he caught on fire and burned;
And he fell to the ground in a heap of ashes.

When he was lying destroyed on the ground,
The ashes drew together, and returned
The soul to its original condition.

Like the great sages confessed,
That when the phoenix dies,
He is born again from the ashes every five
hundred years.
It does not feed on herb or grain in its life,
But on tears of incense and ammonium,
Nard and myrrh are its last winding sheet.

Like a man, who falls without knowing how,
Is forced by demons, who drag him down from
earth,
Or other obstruction that binds man,

When he arises and looks around,
Wholly bewildered by the mighty anguish
Which he has suffered, and while looking sighs;

Such was the sinner after he had risen.
Justice of God! Oh how severe it is,
The punishment that blows like these, pouring
down vengeance!
The Guide asked him who he was;
He replied: "I am from Tuscany
And I have not been here long in this cruel gorge.

I was pleased by a bestial life, not a human one,
And I was like a mule; I'm Vanni Fucci,
Beast and Pistoia were my worthy den."

I told the Guide: "Tell him not to stir,
And ask him what crime has thrust him here
below,
For I saw him before."

Hearing the exchange, the sinner remained,
But he did not look me in the face,
But appeared melancholy and shameful.

Then he said: "It pains me more that you have
caught me here

Amid this misery where thou seest me,
Than when I from the other life was taken.

What thou demandest I cannot deny;
So low am I put down because I robbed
The sacristy of the fair ornaments,

And falsely once 'twas laid upon another;
But that thou mayst not such a sight enjoy,
If thou shalt e'er be out of the dark places,

Thine ears to my announcement ope and hear:
Pistoia first of Neri groweth meagre;
Then Florence doth renew her men and manners;

Mars draws a vapour up from Val di Magra,
Which is with turbid clouds enveloped round,
And with impetuous and bitter tempest

Over Campo Picen shall be the battle;
When it shall suddenly rend the mist asunder,
So that each Bianco shall thereby be smitten.

And this I've said that it may give thee pain."

Amid this misery where you see me now,
So different from when I was taken from the other
life.
What you think I cannot deny;
I am placed so low because I robbed
The sacristy of the fair ornaments,

I also blamed another;
But so you may not enjoy seeing this sight,
If you are ever out of the dark places,

Listen to what I have to say:
Pistoia, grows meager;
While Florence grows stronger in men and
manners;
Mars draws breath from Val di Magra,
Which is with the turbid could envelope around,
And with an impetuous and bitter temper

Will battle over Campo Picen;
When it the mist is blown asunder,
Each Bianco will be smitten.

And I've said this to give you much pain."

Inferno: Canto XXV

At the conclusion of his words, the thief
Lifted his hands aloft with both the figs,
Crying: "Take that, God, for at thee I aim them."

From that time forth the serpents were my friends;

For one entwined itself about his neck
As if it said: "I will not thou speak more;"

And round his arms another, and rebound him,

Clinching itself together so in front,
That with them he could not a motion make.

Pistoia, ah, Pistoia! why resolve not
To burn thyself to ashes and so perish,
Since in ill-doing thou thy seed excellest?

Through all the sombre circles of this Hell,
Spirit I saw not against God so proud,
Not he who fell at Thebes down from the walls!

He fled away, and spake no further word;
And I beheld a Centaur full of rage
Come crying out: "Where is, where is the scoffer?"

I do not think Maremma has so many
Serpents as he had all along his back,
As far as where our countenance begins.

Upon the shoulders, just behind the nape,
With wings wide open was a dragon lying,
And he sets fire to all that he encounters.

My Master said: "That one is Cacus, who
Beneath the rock upon Mount Aventine
Created oftentimes a lake of blood.

He goes not on the same road with his brothers

By reason of the fraudulent theft he made
Of the great herd, which he had near to him;

At the conclusion of his words, the thief
Lifted his hands up and with both fists
Cried: "Take that, God, for I am aiming at you."

From them on, I considered the serpents my
friends;
One entwined itself about his neck,
As if it was saying: "I will not let you speak any
more;"
Another wound itself around his arms, binding
him
In the front,
So he could not move.

Pistoia, oh Pistoia! Why not
Resolve yourself to burn to ashes and perish,
Since, with ill-doing, your children succeed?

Throughout all the somber circles of Hell,
I never saw a spirit go against God so proudly,
Not even the one who tore down the walls of
Thebes!
He fled away and spoke no more;
And I saw a Centaur, filled with rage,
Approaching and crying out: "Where is the
scoffer?"
I don't think Maremma had as many
Serpents along his back,
As far as I could tell.

On his shoulder, just behind the neck,
Was a dragon, lying with open wings,
Setting fire to all he encountered.

My Master said: "That is Cacus, who
Beneath the rock of Mount Aventine
Often created a lake of blood.

He does not go on the same road with his
brothers,
Because he stole
The great herd that was near him;

Whereat his tortuous actions ceased beneath
The mace of Hercules, who peradventure
Gave him a hundred, and he felt not ten."
While he was speaking thus, he had passed by,
And spirits three had underneath us come,
Of which nor I aware was, nor my Leader,

Until what time they shouted: "Who are you?"
On which account our story made a halt,
And then we were intent on them alone.

I did not know them; but it came to pass,
As it is wont to happen by some chance,
That one to name the other was compelled,

Exclaiming: "Where can Cianfa have remained?"
Whence I, so that the Leader might attend,
Upward from chin to nose my finger laid.

If thou art, Reader, slow now to believe
What I shall say, it will no marvel be,
For I who saw it hardly can admit it.

As I was holding raised on them my brows,
Behold! a serpent with six feet darts forth
In front of one, and fastens wholly on him.

With middle feet it bound him round the paunch,
And with the forward ones his arms it seized;
Then thrust its teeth through one cheek and the other;

The hindermost it stretched upon his thighs,
And put its tail through in between the two,
And up behind along the reins outspread it.

Ivy was never fastened by its barbs
Unto a tree so, as this horrible reptile
Upon the other's limbs entwined its own.

Then they stuck close, as if of heated wax
They had been made, and intermixed their colour;
Nor one nor other seemed now what he was;

E'en as proceedeth on before the flame
Upward along the paper a brown colour,
Which is not black as yet, and the white dies.

His torturous actions were stopped
By the mace of Hercules, who
Gave him a hundred whacks, and he only felt ten."
While he was speaking this, he passed by
And three spirits had gathered underneath us,
Unaware to my Leader or me,

Until they shouted: "Who are you?"
Making us stop our story,
So that we focused only on them.

I did not know them; but it just so happened
As it often does,
That one was compelled by the name of the other,

Exclaiming: "Where can Cianfa be?"
Whereupon, so my Leader would see,
Laid my finger across my lips.

If you are slow to believe, Reader,
What I say, it will not be a surprise,
For I hardly believe it myself.

As I was watching,
Behold! A serpent with six feet darted forward
And fastened himself on one.

It bound him around the torso with its middle feet,
And around the arms with its upper ones;
Then it thrust its teeth through his cheeks;

Its rear stretched down his thighs,
And put its tail in between,
Spreading itself along the back.

Ivy never grew as quickly
Along a tree, as this horrible reptile
Entwined itself around his limbs.

Then, like heated wax,
They became one and combined colors;
Neither one seemed as they were;

Like a flame moving
Upward along paper, coloring it brown,
Before it turned black,

The other two looked on, and each of them
Cried out: "O me, Agnello, how thou changest!

Behold, thou now art neither two nor one."

Already the two heads had one become,
When there appeared to us two figures mingled
Into one face, wherein the two were lost.

Of the four lists were fashioned the two arms,
The thighs and legs, the belly and the chest
Members became that never yet were seen.

Every original aspect there was cancelled;
Two and yet none did the perverted image
Appear, and such departed with slow pace.

Even as a lizard, under the great scourge
Of days canicular, exchanging hedge,
Lightning appeareth if the road it cross;

Thus did appear, coming towards the bellies
Of the two others, a small fiery serpent,
Livid and black as is a peppercorn.

And in that part whereat is first received
Our aliment, it one of them transfixed;
Then downward fell in front of him extended.

The one transfixed looked at it, but said naught;
Nay, rather with feet motionless he yawned,
Just as if sleep or fever had assailed him.

He at the serpent gazed, and it at him;
One through the wound, the other through the mouth
Smoked violently, and the smoke commingled.

Henceforth be silent Lucan, where he mentions
Wretched Sabellus and Nassidius,
And wait to hear what now shall be shot forth.

Be silent Ovid, of Cadmus and Arethusa;
For if him to a snake, her to fountain,

Converts he fabling, that I grudge him not;

Because two natures never front to front

---

*The other two looked on and
Cried out: "Oh me, Agnello! How you are
changing!
Look, you are neither human nor serpent."*

*Already the two heads became one,
When the two figures mingled
Into one.*

*Four arms turned into two,
The thighs, legs, belly, and chest
Were like something never seen.*

*So, every original body part was cancelled;
Starting out as two, the final image appeared
Perverted and slowly.*

*Like a lizard, under the great torment
Of the days of old, changed
With the appearance of lightning as it crossed the
road;*

*Similarly, coming towards the bellies
Of the two others was a small fiery serpent,
Angry and black as peppercorn.*

*And just like before,
It transfixed one of them,
Falling down prostrate in front of him.*

*The transfixed spirit looked at it, but said nothing;
Rather with motionless feet, he yawned,
As if sleep or fever had struck him.*

*Gazing at the serpent and him;
One wound through the mouth
Smoking violently.*

*Now, be silent Lucan, where he mentioned
The wretched Sabellus and Nassidius,
And wait to hear what happened next.*

*Be silent Ovid, of Cadmus and Arethusa;
Whether the transformation of man into snake or
woman into water,
I am not lying;*

Because there never were two creatures

Has he transmuted, so that both the forms
To interchange their matter ready were.

Together they responded in such wise,
That to a fork the serpent cleft his tail
And eke the wounded drew his feet together.

The legs together with the thighs themselves
Adhered so, that in little time the juncture
No sign whatever made that was apparent.

He with the cloven tail assumed the figure
The other one was losing, and his skin
Became elastic, and the other's hard.

I saw the arms draw inward at the armpits,
And both feet of the reptile, that were short,
Lengthen as much as those contracted were.

Thereafter the hind feet, together twisted,
Became the member that a man conceals,
And of his own the wretch had two created.

While both of them the exhalation veils
With a new colour, and engenders hair
On one of them and depilates the other,

The one uprose and down the other fell,
Though turning not away their impious lamps,
Underneath which each one his muzzle changed.

He who was standing drew it tow'rds the temples,
And from excess of matter, which came thither,
Issued the ears from out the hollow cheeks;

What did not backward run and was retained
Of that excess made to the face a nose,
And the lips thickened far as was befitting.

He who lay prostrate thrusts his muzzle forward,

And backward draws the ears into his head,
In the same manner as the snail its horns;

And so the tongue, which was entire and apt
For speech before, is cleft, and the bi-forked
In the other closes up, and the smoke ceases.

So transmuted that both the forms
Interchanged readily and completely.

Together they responded,
With the serpent forking his tail,
Causing the spirit to draw his feet together.

The legs and thighs adhered
Together, in just a short time,
With no apparent sign made.

He with the cloven tail assumed the figure,
The other one was losing, and his skin
Became elastic, and the other's hard.

I saw the arms draw inward at the armpits,
And both short feet of the reptile
Lengthened as much as the contracted ones.

Afterwards the hind feet, twisted together,
Becoming the man's private parts,
Creating two for himself.

While both of them revealed with deep breath,
A new color, One grew hair,
And the other lost it,

One rose up and the other fell down,
Without closing their eyes,
Each one's face transformed.

He who was standing drew it towards the temples,
And from the excess of matter,
Fashioned ears from hollow cheeks;

What was left,
Made a nose,
And thickened the lips.

He, who was lying on the ground thrust his face
forward,
And his ears withdrew into his head,
Like the horns of a snail.

His tongue, which was meant
For speech became cleft and forked,
While the other's closed up and the smoke
stopped.

The soul, which to a reptile had been changed,
Along the valley hissing takes to flight,
And after him the other speaking sputters.

Then did he turn upon him his new shoulders,
And said to the other: "I'll have Buoso run,
Crawling as I have done, along this road."

In this way I beheld the seventh ballast
Shift and reshift, and here be my excuse
The novelty, if aught my pen transgress.

And notwithstanding that mine eyes might be
Somewhat bewildered, and my mind dismayed,
They could not flee away so secretly

But that I plainly saw Puccio Sciancato;
And he it was who sole of three companions,
Which came in the beginning, was not changed;

The other was he whom thou, Gaville, weepest.

The soul, which changed to a reptile,
Took to the valley, hissing,
And the other began to speak.

Turning his new shoulders,
He said to the other: "I'll have Buoso run,
Since all I have done is crawl along this road."

In this way, I saw the seventh ballast
Shift and reshift, and let me provide an excuse,
If my pen cannot transgress the novelty.

My eyes were somewhat bewildered
And my mind dismayed,
So they could not escape

What I plainly saw, Puccio Sciancato;
Who came with the three companions
Was not changed.

The other was the one for whom Gaville wept.

Inferno: Canto XXVI

Rejoice, O Florence, since thou art so great,
That over sea and land thou beatest thy wings,
And throughout Hell thy name is spread abroad!

Among the thieves five citizens of thine
Like these I found, whence shame comes unto me,
And thou thereby to no great honour risest.

But if when morn is near our dreams are true,

Feel shalt thou in a little time from now
What Prato, if none other, craves for thee.

And if it now were, it were not too soon;
Would that it were, seeing it needs must be,
For 'twill aggrieve me more the more I age.

We went our way, and up along the stairs
The bourns had made us to descend before,
Remounted my Conductor and drew me.

And following the solitary path
Among the rocks and ridges of the crag,
The foot without the hand sped not at all.

Then sorrowed I, and sorrow now again,
When I direct my mind to what I saw,
And more my genius curb than I am wont,

That it may run not unless virtue guide it;
So that if some good star, or better thing,
Have given me good, I may myself not grudge it.

As many as the hind (who on the hill
Rests at the time when he who lights the world
His countenance keeps least concealed from us,

While as the fly gives place unto the gnat)
Seeth the glow-worms down along the valley,

Perchance there where he ploughs and makes his vintage;
With flames as manifold resplendent all

Rejoice, oh Florence, since you were so great,
That over sea and land you beat your wings,
And throughout Hell, your name was spread!

Among the thieves, five citizens of yours
Were found, which shamed me,
So you are not given much honor.

But if when the morning is near and our dreams
were true,
You will feel in a little time from now
What Prato said, if no one else craved it or you.

And if it were now, it would not be too soon;
I wish it were, if it must be,
Because it will harm me more as I grow older.

We went our way up the stairs
We had descended before,
And I remounted my Conductor, who held me
closely.
Following the solitary path
Among the rocks and ridges of the crag,
We sped along.

Then I was overcome with sorrow, as I am now,
When I think about what I saw,
Which I try not to remember more than necessary,

But as virtue demands,
So, if some good star or better thing
Gives me good fortune, I may not deny it.

As many as the hind, (who rest on the hill,
When he, who lights the world,
Keeps his countenance concealed from us the
least,
While the fly gives place to the gnat)
Seeing the glow-worm down along the valley,

By chance where he ploughs and makes his wine;
With resplendent flames I became aware

Was the eighth Bolgia, as I grew aware
As soon as I was where the depth appeared.

And such as he who with the bears avenged him
Beheld Elijah's chariot at departing,
What time the steeds to heaven erect uprose,

For with his eye he could not follow it
So as to see aught else than flame alone,
Even as a little cloud ascending upward,

Thus each along the gorge of the intrenchment
Was moving; for not one reveals the theft,
And every flame a sinner steals away.

I stood upon the bridge uprisen to see,
So that, if I had seized not on a rock,
Down had I fallen without being pushed.

And the Leader, who beheld me so attent,
Exclaimed: "Within the fires the spirits are;
Each swathes himself with that wherewith he burns."

"My Master," I replied, "by hearing thee

I am more sure; but I surmised already
It might be so, and already wished to ask thee

Who is within that fire, which comes so cleft

At top, it seems uprising from the pyre
Where was Eteocles with his brother placed."

He answered me: "Within there are tormented
Ulysses and Diomed, and thus together
They unto vengeance run as unto wrath.

And there within their flame do they lament
The ambush of the horse, which made the door
Whence issued forth the Romans' gentle seed;

Therein is wept the craft, for which being dead
Deidamia still deplores Achilles,
And pain for the Palladium there is borne."

"If they within those sparks possess the power
To speak," I said, "thee, Master, much I pray,
And re-pray, that the prayer be worth a thousand,

Of the eighth Bolgia,
As soon as I was where the depth appeared.

Like he, who was avenged by the bears
Saw Elijah's chariot departing,
When the steeds rose up towards heaven,

For with his eye he could not follow it,
Seeing nothing but the lone flame,
As a little cloud ascended upward,

Thus, along the gorge of the trench
Was moving; Revealing no thieves,
A flame concealed a sinner.

I stood upon the bridge to see,
So that, if I had not seized not a rock,
I would have fallen down.

And the Leader, who watched me so attentively,
Exclaimed: "The spirits are within the fires;
Each swathes himself wherever he burns."

"My Master," I replied, "I am not sure, I'm hearing you right,
But I already surmised that
It may be so, and I want to ask you

Who is within the fire, which burns with two flames
At the top; it seems to be rising up from the pyre
Where Eteocles was placed with his brother."

He answered: "There are two tormented souls,
Ulysses and Diomed, who burn in wrath
Like they sought vengeance.

Within the flame they lament
The ambush of the horse, which made the door
For the Roman's gentle seed;

They weep for the craft, which made dead
Deidamia deplore Achilles,
And bore the pain for the Palladium.

"If they, within those sparks, can speak,"
I said, "I wish very much,
That you would proceed

That thou make no denial of awaiting
Until the horned flame shall hither come;
Thou seest that with desire I lean towards it."

And he to me: "Worthy is thy entreaty
Of much applause, and therefore I accept it;
But take heed that thy tongue restrain itself.

Leave me to speak, because I have conceived
That which thou wishest; for they might disdain
Perchance, since they were Greeks, discourse of thine."

When now the flame had come unto that point,
Where to my Leader it seemed time and place,
After this fashion did I hear him speak:

"O ye, who are twofold within one fire,
If I deserved of you, while I was living,
If I deserved of you or much or little

When in the world I wrote the lofty verses,
Do not move on, but one of you declare
Whither, being lost, he went away to die."

Then of the antique flame the greater horn,
Murmuring, began to wave itself about
Even as a flame doth which the wind fatigues.

Thereafterward, the summit to and fro
Moving as if it were the tongue that spake,
It uttered forth a voice, and said: "When I

From Circe had departed, who concealed me
More than a year there near unto Gaeta,
Or ever yet Aeneas named it so,

Nor fondness for my son, nor reverence
For my old father, nor the due affection
Which joyous should have made Penelope,

Could overcome within me the desire
I had to be experienced of the world,
And of the vice and virtue of mankind;

But I put forth on the high open sea
With one sole ship, and that small company
By which I never had deserted been.

Without waiting
Until the horned flame comes here;
I'm practically leaning towards them."

He replied: "Your request is worthy
Of much applause, and therefore I accept it;
But take heed that you refrain from speaking.

Let me speak for you, because I know
What you want; and they may have disdain
For you, since they were Greeks, enemies of
yours."
When the flame had come to the point,
Where my Leader thought it appropriate,
He spoke:

"Oh you, who burn together in the fire,
If I deserved your friendship while I was living,
Whether a lot or a little

When I wrote the lofty verses in the world,
Don't move on, but one of you declare
How you died."

Out of the antique flame the older soul,
Murmuring, began to wave itself about
Like a flame blown in the wind.

Thereafter, he arose to the summit
Moving as if he were a tongue,
And uttered forth: "When I

Departed from Circe, where I hid
More than a year, near Gaeta,
As Aeneas named it,

Neither fondness for my son, nor reverence
For my old father, or the affection
Which joyous Penelope would have made

Could overcome the desire within
To experience the world,
Born of the vice and virtue of mankind;

So I went out on the high open sea
With one lone ship, and that small company
Which was always loyal to me.

Both of the shores I saw as far as Spain,
Far as Morocco, and the isle of Sardes,
And the others which that sea bathes round about.

I and my company were old and slow
When at that narrow passage we arrived
Where Hercules his landmarks set as signals,

That man no farther onward should adventure.
On the right hand behind me left I Seville,
And on the other already had left Ceuta.

'O brothers, who amid a hundred thousand
Perils,' I said, 'have come unto the West,
To this so inconsiderable vigil

Which is remaining of your senses still
Be ye unwilling to deny the knowledge,
Following the sun, of the unpeopled world.

Consider ye the seed from which ye sprang;
Ye were not made to live like unto brutes,
But for pursuit of virtue and of knowledge.'

So eager did I render my companions,
With this brief exhortation, for the voyage,
That then I hardly could have held them back.

And having turned our stern unto the morning,
We of the oars made wings for our mad flight,
Evermore gaining on the larboard side.

Already all the stars of the other pole
The night beheld, and ours so very low
It did not rise above the ocean floor.

Five times rekindled and as many quenched
Had been the splendour underneath the moon,
Since we had entered into the deep pass,

When there appeared to us a mountain, dim
From distance, and it seemed to me so high
As I had never any one beheld.

Joyful were we, and soon it turned to weeping;
For out of the new land a whirlwind rose,
And smote upon the fore part of the ship.

I saw both of the shores as far as Spain,
As far as Morocco, and the isle of Sardes,
And the other areas bathed by that sea.

My company and I were old and slow
When we arrived at that narrow passage
Where Hercules used landmarks to signal

Men to go no farther on adventure.
On the right hand, I left Seville behind,
And on the other, Cueta.

'Oh brothers, who amid a hundred thousand
Perils,' I said, 'have come to the west,
To this inconsiderable vigil,

Which if your senses still remain
Do not be willing to deny the knowledge
Of the world by following the sun.'

Consider the seed you came from
You were not made to live like violent people
But to chase virtue and knowledge

I rendered my companions eager,
With this brief speech, for the voyage,
That I could hardly have held them back.

And having turned our stern unto the morning,
We made our oars wings for the mad flight,
Gaining evermore on the larboard side.

Already all the stars of the other pole
Beheld the night, and ours was so very low
It did not rise above the ocean floor.

We had spent five nights
Under the splendor of the moon,
Since we had entered into the deep pass,

When a mountain dimly appeared to us
From a distance, and it seemed to me higher
Than any I had ever seen.

We were joyful, and we soon turned to weeping;
For out of the new land a whirlwind rose,
And struck the front part of the ship.

Three times it made her whirl with all the waters,
At the fourth time it made the stern uplift,
And the prow downward go, as pleased Another,

Until the sea above us closed again."

It made her whirl three times with all the waters,
So during the fourth, the stern uplifted and
The prow went downward, as God deemed,

Until the sea closed above us again."

Inferno: Canto XXVII

Already was the flame erect and quiet,
To speak no more, and now departed from us
With the permission of the gentle Poet;

When yet another, which behind it came,
Caused us to turn our eyes upon its top
By a confused sound that issued from it.

As the Sicilian bull (that bellowed first
With the lament of him, and that was right,
Who with his file had modulated it)

Bellowed so with the voice of the afflicted,
That, notwithstanding it was made of brass,
Still it appeared with agony transfixed;

Thus, by not having any way or issue
At first from out the fire, to its own language
Converted were the melancholy words.

But afterwards, when they had gathered way
Up through the point, giving it that vibration
The tongue had given them in their passage out,

We heard it said: "O thou, at whom I aim
My voice, and who but now wast speaking Lombard,
Saying, 'Now go thy way, no more I urge thee,'

Because I come perchance a little late,
To stay and speak with me let it not irk thee;
Thou seest it irks not me, and I am burning.

If thou but lately into this blind world
Hast fallen down from that sweet Latian land,
Wherefrom I bring the whole of my transgression,

Say, if the Romagnuols have peace or war.

For I was from the mountains there between
Urbino and the yoke whence Tiber bursts."

I still was downward bent and listening,

Already the flame was erect and quiet,
Departing from us, without speaking
As permitted by the gentle Poet;

When another, from behind it, came
Causing us to turn our eyes upon its top
By a confused sound that issued from it.

As the Sicilian bull (that first bellowed
With the lament of him, who
Had modeled it with his file)

So the voice bellowed like one of the afflicted,
Like it was made of brass,
It appeared, transfixed with agony;

Thus, by not having any way
Out of the fire, it converted to its own language
With melancholy words.

Afterwards, when they had gathered way
Up through the point, giving utterance
Like the tongue had given them in their passage
out,
We heard: "Oh you, at whom I aim
My voice, and who was now just saying,
'Now go your way, no more I urge you,'

Because I come perhaps a little late,
Do not let it bother you to stay and speak with me;
You see it does not irk me, and I am burning.

If you are just arriving into this blind world,
Having fallen down from that sweet Latin land,
From where I bring the whole of my transgression,

Please tell me, if the Romagnuols have peace or
war,
For I was from the mountains there between
Urbino and the place where the Tiber bursts
forth."

I was still bent downward listening,

When my Conductor touched me on the side,
Saying: "Speak thou: this one a Latian is."

And I, who had beforehand my reply
In readiness, forthwith began to speak:
"O soul, that down below there art concealed,

Romagna thine is not and never has been
Without war in the bosom of its tyrants;
But open war I none have left there now.

Ravenna stands as it long years has stood;
The Eagle of Polenta there is brooding,
So that she covers Cervia with her vans.

The city which once made the long resistance,
And of the French a sanguinary heap,
Beneath the Green Paws finds itself again;

Verrucchio's ancient Mastiff and the new,
Who made such bad disposal of Montagna,
Where they are wont make wimbles of their teeth.

The cities of Lamone and Santerno
Governs the Lioncel of the white lair,
Who changes sides 'twixt summer-time and winter;

And that of which the Savio bathes the flank,
Even as it lies between the plain and mountain,
Lives between tyranny and a free state.

Now I entreat thee tell us who thou art;
Be not more stubborn than the rest have been,
So may thy name hold front there in the world."

After the fire a little more had roared
In its own fashion, the sharp point it moved
This way and that, and then gave forth such breath:

"If I believed that my reply were made
To one who to the world would e'er return,
This flame without more flickering would stand still;

But inasmuch as never from this depth
Did any one return, if I hear true,
Without the fear of infamy I answer,

I was a man of arms, then Cordelier,

When my Conductor touched me on the side,
Saying: "Speak you: this one is Latin."

And I, who had my reply ready before,
Began to speak:
"Oh soul, that are concealed down here,

Your Romagna is not and never has been
Without war in the bosom of its tyrants;
But there is no open war there now.

Ravenna stands as it has stood for many years;
The Eagle of Polenta is brooding there,
So that she covers Cervia.

The city which once made the long resistance,
And turned the French into a sanguinary heap,
Finds itself beneath the Green Paws again;

Verrucchio's ancient and new Mastiff,
Who disposed of Montagna,
Causing them to make instruments of their teeth.

The cities of Lamone and Santerno
Governs the Lioncel of the white lair,
Who changes sides between the time of summer
and winter;
And Savio which bathes the flank,
As it lies between the plain and the mountain,
Lives between tyranny and a free state.

Now I ask you to tell us who you are;
Do not be more stubborn than the rest have been,
So your name may be known in the world."

After the fire had roared a little more
In its own fashion, it moved the sharp point
This way and that, and then gave forth such
breath:
"If I believed that my reply was given
To someone who would return to the world,
This flame would stand still with no more
flickering;
But since none has ever returned from this depth,
As I have been told,
Without the fear of infamy, I answer,

I was a man of arms named Cordelier,

Believing thus begirt to make amends; And truly my belief had been fulfilled	*Who believed I was supposed to make amends* *And my belief had been truly fulfilled*
But for the High Priest, whom may ill betide, Who put me back into my former sins; And how and wherefore I will have thee hear.	*But for the High Priest, whom I hope is ill,* *Who put me back into my former sinful ways;* *I will have you hear how and where.*
While I was still the form of bone and pulp My mother gave to me, the deeds I did Were not those of a lion, but a fox.	*While I was still the form of bone and pulp* *My mother gave to me the traits* *Of a fox, not a lion.*
The machinations and the covert ways I knew them all, and practised so their craft, That to the ends of earth the sound went forth.	*I knew all the machinations and covert ways,* *And practiced their craft so,* *That the sound went to the ends of the earth.*
When now unto that portion of mine age I saw myself arrived, when each one ought To lower the sails, and coil away the ropes,	*When I had arrived at the proper age,* *When each one should* *Lower his sail and coil away the ropes,*
That which before had pleased me then displeased me; And penitent and confessing I surrendered, Ah woe is me! and it would have bestead me;	*That which had pleased me before, displeased me;* *So with penitence I confessed and surrendered,* *Ah woe is me! I would have succeeded;*
The Leader of the modern Pharisees Having a war near unto Lateran, And not with Saracens nor with the Jews,	*The Leader of the modern Pharisees,* *Having a war near Lateran,* *And not with the Saracens or the Jews,*
For each one of his enemies was Christian, And none of them had been to conquer Acre, Nor merchandising in the Sultan's land,	*For each one of his enemies was Christian,* *And none of them had been to conquer Acre,* *Nor trade in the Sultan's land,*
Nor the high office, nor the sacred orders, In him regarded, nor in me that cord Which used to make those girt with it more meagre;	*Or the high office or the sacred orders,* *That cord, which makes men meager* *Did not reside within him or me;*
But even as Constantine sought out Sylvester To cure his leprosy, within Soracte, So this one sought me out as an adept	*But like Constantine sought out Sylvester* *To cure his leprosy, within Soracte,* *This one sought me out as an advisor*
To cure him of the fever of his pride. Counsel he asked of me, and I was silent, Because his words appeared inebriate.	*To cure him of the fever of his pride.* *He asked me for counsel, and I was silent,* *Because his words appeared confusing.*
And then he said: 'Be not thy heart afraid; Henceforth I thee absolve; and thou instruct me How to raze Palestrina to the ground.	*Then he said: 'Do not be afraid;* *I absolve you; and now you instruct me* *How to conquer Palestrina.*
Heaven have I power to lock and to unlock,	*I have the power to lock and unlock Heaven,*

As thou dost know; therefore the keys are two,
The which my predecessor held not dear.'

Then urged me on his weighty arguments
There, where my silence was the worst advice;
And said I: 'Father, since thou washest me

Of that sin into which I now must fall,
The promise long with the fulfilment short
Will make thee triumph in thy lofty seat.'

Francis came afterward, when I was dead,
For me; but one of the black Cherubim
Said to him: 'Take him not; do me no wrong;

He must come down among my servitors,
Because he gave the fraudulent advice
From which time forth I have been at his hair;

For who repents not cannot be absolved,
Nor can one both repent and will at once,
Because of the contradiction which consents not.'

O miserable me! how I did shudder
When he seized on me, saying: 'Peradventure
Thou didst not think that I was a logician!'

He bore me unto Minos, who entwined
Eight times his tail about his stubborn back,
And after he had bitten it in great rage,

Said: 'Of the thievish fire a culprit this;'
Wherefore, here where thou seest, am I lost,
And vested thus in going I bemoan me."

When it had thus completed its recital,
The flame departed uttering lamentations,
Writhing and flapping its sharp-pointed horn.

Onward we passed, both I and my Conductor,
Up o'er the crag above another arch,
Which the moat covers, where is paid the fee

By those who, sowing discord, win their burden.

As you know; therefore there are two keys,
Which my predecessor did not hold dear.'

Then with his weighty arguments, he urged me,
Where my silence was the worst advice;
And I said: 'Father, since you washed me

Of that sin into which I now must fall,
The long promise with the short fulfillment
Will make you triumph in your lofty seat.'

St. Francis came after men, when I was dead;
But one of the black Cherubim
Said to him, 'Do not take him; do not wrong me;

He must come down among my servants,
Because he gave fraudulent advice
From which time I have been here;

For he who does not repent cannot be absolved,
Nor can one both repent and continue to sin,
Because of the contradiction not consented.'

Oh miserable me! How I did shudder
When he seized on me, saying: 'By chance
Did you not think I was a logician!'

He took me to Minos, who entwined
His tail eight times around his stubborn back,
And after he had bitten it in great rage,

Said: 'This culprit is of the thievish fire;'
Wherefore, I was sent here,
To moan for myself."

When it had completed its recital,
The flame departed uttering lamentations,
Writhing and flapping its sharp-pointed horn.

My Conductor and I passed onward,
Up over the crag above another arch,
Which the moat covered, and where the fee is paid

By those who, sowing discord, win their burden.

Inferno: Canto XXVIII

Who ever could, e'en with untrammelled words,
Tell of the blood and of the wounds in full
Which now I saw, by many times narrating?

Each tongue would for a certainty fall short
By reason of our speech and memory,
That have small room to comprehend so much.

If were again assembled all the people
Which formerly upon the fateful land
Of Puglia were lamenting for their blood

Shed by the Romans and the lingering war
That of the rings made such illustrious spoils,
As Livy has recorded, who errs not,

With those who felt the agony of blows
By making counterstand to Robert Guiscard,
And all the rest, whose bones are gathered still

At Ceperano, where a renegade
Was each Apulian, and at Tagliacozzo,
Where without arms the old Alardo conquered,

And one his limb transpierced, and one lopped off,

Should show, it would be nothing to compare
With the disgusting mode of the ninth Bolgia.

A cask by losing centre-piece or cant
Was never shattered so, as I saw one
Rent from the chin to where one breaketh wind.

Between his legs were hanging down his entrails;
His heart was visible, and the dismal sack
That maketh excrement of what is eaten.

While I was all absorbed in seeing him,
He looked at me, and opened with his hands
His bosom, saying: "See now how I rend me;

How mutilated, see, is Mahomet;

Who could even with untrammeled words,
Relate the blood and wounds,
Which now I saw?

Each tongue would certainly fall short,
Either by speech or memory,
That do not have the room to comprehend so
much.
If the people were all assembled,
Who formerly lived upon the land
Of Puglia, lamenting for their blood

Shed by the Romans and the lingering war
That made such illustrious spoils,
As Livy, who never errs, recorded,

With those who felt the agony of blows
By making a counter stand to Robert Guiscard,
And all the rest, whose bones are still gathered

At Ceperano, where a renegade
Was at Apulian and Tagliacozzo,
Where without arms the old Alardo conquered

With one of his limbs was pierced, and one lopped
off,
Showing it would be nothing compared
With the disgusting mode of the ninth Bolgia.

A cask was never shattered,
By losing its center piece, as I saw one soul
Split from chin to tail.

His entrails were hanging between his legs;
His heart was visible, as was the dismal sack
That makes excrement of what is eaten.

While I was completely absorbed in seeing him,
He looked at me, and with open hands
His bosom saying: "See now how I rend me;

How mutilated, see, Mahomet;

In front of me doth Ali weeping go,
Cleft in the face from forelock unto chin;

And all the others whom thou here beholdest,
Disseminators of scandal and of schism
While living were, and therefore are cleft thus.

A devil is behind here, who doth cleave us
Thus cruelly, unto the falchion's edge
Putting again each one of all this ream,

When we have gone around the doleful road;
By reason that our wounds are closed again
Ere any one in front of him repass.

But who art thou, that musest on the crag,
Perchance to postpone going to the pain
That is adjudged upon thine accusations?"

"Nor death hath reached him yet, nor guilt doth
bring him,"
My Master made reply, "to be tormented;
But to procure him full experience,

Me, who am dead, behoves it to conduct him
Down here through Hell, from circle unto circle;
And this is true as that I speak to thee."

More than a hundred were there when they heard him,
Who in the moat stood still to look at me,
Through wonderment oblivious of their torture.

"Now say to Fra Dolcino, then, to arm him,
Thou, who perhaps wilt shortly see the sun,
If soon he wish not here to follow me,

So with provisions, that no stress of snow
May give the victory to the Novarese,
Which otherwise to gain would not be easy."

After one foot to go away he lifted,
This word did Mahomet say unto me,
Then to depart upon the ground he stretched it.

Another one, who had his throat pierced through,
And nose cut off close underneath the brows,
And had no longer but a single ear,

In front of me Ali goes weeping,
Cleft in the face from scalp to chin;

And all the others whom you see,
Were disseminators of scandal and division
While living, are also split.

A devil is behind here, who cleaves us
So cruelly, with the edge of his sword
Putting each one of us together again,

When we go around the doleful road;
Our wounds close again
Before we pass in front of him.

But who are you, that watches from the crag,
Perhaps hoping to postpone going to the pain
That is your judgment?"

"Neither death nor guilt has
brought him here,"
My Master replied, "To be tormented;
He is here to experience Hell in full,

And I, who am dead, is his conductor
From circle to circle down through Hell;
And this is the truth."

More than a hundred heard him,
Who stood still in the moat and looked at me,
With wonderment and oblivion of their torture.

"Then say to Fra Dolcino, to arm him,
You, who perhaps will shortly see the sun,
If he does not wish to follow me,

So with provisions, that no stress of snow
May give the Noavese the victory,
Which would otherwise not be easy to gain."

After he lifted one foot to go away,
Mahomet said this to me,
Stretching his leg upon the ground.

Another one with a pierced throat,
And nose cut off,
With only one ear,

Staying to look in wonder with the others, Before the others did his gullet open, Which outwardly was red in every part,	*Stayed with the others looking in awe, Before the others opened his gullet, Which bled red outwardly*
And said: "O thou, whom guilt doth not condemn, And whom I once saw up in Latian land, Unless too great similitude deceive me, Call to remembrance Pier da Medicina, If e'er thou see again the lovely plain That from Vercelli slopes to Marcabo,	*Saying: "You, whom guilt does not condemn, I saw up in Latian land once, Unless similitude deceives me, Try to remember Pier da Medicina, If you ever see the lovely plain again That slope from Vercelli to Marcabo,*
And make it known to the best two of Fano, To Messer Guido and Angiolello likewise, That if foreseeing here be not in vain,	*Make it known to the two best of Fano, Messer Guido and Angiolello, That if foreseeing here is true,*
Cast over from their vessel shall they be, And drowned near unto the Cattolica, By the betrayal of a tyrant fell.	*They will be cast over from their vessel, And drowned near the Cattolica, By the betrayal of a fallen tyrant.*
Between the isles of Cyprus and Majorca Neptune ne'er yet beheld so great a crime, Neither of pirates nor Argolic people.	*Between the isles of Cyprus and Majorca Neptune never beheld so great a crime, By neither the pirates nor the Argolic people.*
That traitor, who sees only with one eye, And holds the land, which some one here with me Would fain be fasting from the vision of,	*That traitor, who sees with only one eye, And holds the land, which someone here with me, Had the vision,*
Will make them come unto a parley with him; Then will do so, that to Focara's wind	*Will make them come into parley with him; Then will betray them so, according to Focara's wind*
They will not stand in need of vow or prayer."	*They will not stand in need of prayer."*
And I to him: "Show to me and declare, If thou wouldst have me bear up news of thee, Who is this person of the bitter vision."	*I replied: "Show to me and swear, Who the person is that had this vision, If you want me to take the news from you."*
Then did he lay his hand upon the jaw Of one of his companions, and his mouth Oped, crying: "This is he, and he speaks not.	*Then he laid his hand upon the jaw Of one of his companions, opening his mouth Cried: "This is he, but he won't speak.*
This one, being banished, every doubt submerged	*This one, having been banished, submerged every doubt*
In Caesar by affirming the forearmed Always with detriment allowed delay."	*In Caesar by affirming the forearmed And always with detriment allowed delay."*
O how bewildered unto me appeared, With tongue asunder in his windpipe slit, Curio, who in speaking was so bold!	*Oh how bewildered he appeared to me, With his tongue asunder and his windpipe slit, Curio, so bold in speaking!*

And one, who both his hands dissevered had,
The stumps uplifting through the murky air,
So that the blood made horrible his face,

Cried out: "Thou shalt remember Mosca also,
Who said, alas! 'A thing done has an end!'
Which was an ill seed for the Tuscan people."

"And death unto thy race," thereto I added;
Whence he, accumulating woe on woe,
Departed, like a person sad and crazed.

But I remained to look upon the crowd;
And saw a thing which I should be afraid,
Without some further proof, even to recount,

If it were not that conscience reassures me,
That good companion which emboldens man
Beneath the hauberk of its feeling pure.

I truly saw, and still I seem to see it,
A trunk without a head walk in like manner
As walked the others of the mournful herd.

And by the hair it held the head dissevered,
Hung from the hand in fashion of a lantern,
And that upon us gazed and said: "O me!"

It of itself made to itself a lamp,
And they were two in one, and one in two;
How that can be, He knows who so ordains it.

When it was come close to the bridge's foot,
It lifted high its arm with all the head,
To bring more closely unto us its words,

Which were: "Behold now the sore penalty,
Thou, who dost breathing go the dead beholding;
Behold if any be as great as this.

And so that thou may carry news of me,
Know that Bertram de Born am I, the same
Who gave to the Young King the evil comfort.

I made the father and the son rebellious;
Achitophel not more with Absalom
And David did with his accursed goadings.

And one, who had his hands severed,
Lifting up the stumps through the murky air,
So that the blood made his face horrible,

Cried out: "You will remember Mosca also,
Who said, 'A thing done has an end'
Which was an ill seed for the Tuscan people."

"And death to your race," I added;
When he, his woes accumulating,
Departed like a sad, crazed person.

But I remained to look upon the crowd;
And saw a thing which I am afraid to recount
Without further proof,

If it were not that conscience reassures me,
That good companion which emboldens man
Making the feeling pure.

I truly saw, and can still see it,
A body without a head walk in the same manner
As the others in the mournful herd.

It held the severed head by the hair,
Hanging like a lantern,
And said: "Oh me!"

It carried its head like a lamp,
They were two in one;
And how that can be, only the one who ordained it
knows.
When it was close to the bridge's foot,
It lifted its arm with the head high
To bring his words more closely

Which were: "Behold now the sore penalty,
You, who are breathing that go before the dead;
See if any be as great at this.

So you may carry the news of me,
Know that I am Bertram de Born,
Who gave evil comfort to the Young King.

I made the father and the son rebellious;
Like Achitophel with Absalom
And David, with his accursed goading.

Because I parted persons so united,
Parted do I now bear my brain, alas!
From its beginning, which is in this trunk.

Thus is observed in me the counterpoise."

Because I parted people who were so united,
I bear my parted head, alas!
From its beginning which is the trunk.

Thus I observed the balance of justice."

Inferno: Canto XXIX

The many people and the divers wounds
These eyes of mine had so inebriated,
That they were wishful to stand still and weep;

But said Virgilius: "What dost thou still gaze at?
Why is thy sight still riveted down there
Among the mournful, mutilated shades?

Thou hast not done so at the other Bolge;
Consider, if to count them thou believest,
That two-and-twenty miles the valley winds,

And now the moon is underneath our feet;
Henceforth the time allotted us is brief,
And more is to be seen than what thou seest."

"If thou hadst," I made answer thereupon,
"Attended to the cause for which I looked,
Perhaps a longer stay thou wouldst have pardoned."

Meanwhile my Guide departed, and behind him
I went, already making my reply,
And superadding: "In that cavern where

I held mine eyes with such attention fixed,
I think a spirit of my blood laments
The sin which down below there costs so much."

Then said the Master: "Be no longer broken
Thy thought from this time forward upon him;
Attend elsewhere, and there let him remain;

For him I saw below the little bridge,
Pointing at thee, and threatening with his finger

Fiercely, and heard him called Geri del Bello.

So wholly at that time wast thou impeded
By him who formerly held Altaforte,
Thou didst not look that way; so he departed."

"O my Conductor, his own violent death,

The many wounded people
I saw with these eyes of mine
Were still wishful as they stood weeping;

But Virgilius said: "What are you looking at?
Why are you still riveted by what you see,
Among the mournful, mutilated souls?

You did not stare at the other Bolges;
Consider this, if you want to see everything,
About twenty-two miles of winding valleys,

We have already been here for long enough;
Our time is brief,
And there is so much more to be seen."

"If you had," I responded,
"Seen what I just saw,
Perhaps you would have pardoned a longer stay."

Meanwhile, my Guide departed
And I went behind him,
Saying: "In that cavern where

I focused my eyes,
I think a relative of mine laments
The sin which is so costly down there."

Then the Master said: "Don't worry any longer
About what you saw;
Focus on what you are about to see, and let him
remain there;
For I saw him below the little bridge,
Pointing at you, and fiercely threatening with his
finger,
The one called Geri del Bello.

You were so preoccupied at the time
With he, who formerly held Altaforte,
You didn't look that way, so he departed."

"Oh my Conductor, his violent death,

Which is not yet avenged for him," I said,
"By any who is sharer in the shame,

Made him disdainful; whence he went away,
As I imagine, without speaking to me,
And thereby made me pity him the more."

Thus did we speak as far as the first place
Upon the crag, which the next valley shows
Down to the bottom, if there were more light.

When we were now right over the last cloister
Of Malebolge, so that its lay-brothers
Could manifest themselves unto our sight,

Divers lamentings pierced me through and through,
Which with compassion had their arrows barbed,
Whereat mine ears I covered with my hands.

What pain would be, if from the hospitals
Of Valdichiana, 'twixt July and September,
And of Maremma and Sardinia

All the diseases in one moat were gathered,
Such was it here, and such a stench came from it
As from putrescent limbs is wont to issue.

We had descended on the furthest bank
From the long crag, upon the left hand still,
And then more vivid was my power of sight

Down tow'rds the bottom, where the ministress
Of the high Lord, Justice infallible,
Punishes forgers, which she here records.

I do not think a sadder sight to see
Was in Aegina the whole people sick,
(When was the air so full of pestilence,

The animals, down to the little worm,
All fell, and afterwards the ancient people,
According as the poets have affirmed,

Were from the seed of ants restored again,)
Than was it to behold through that dark valley
The spirits languishing in divers heaps.

This on the belly, that upon the back

Which has not yet been avenged," I said,
"By any who share the shame,

Made him disdainful; When he went away,
As I imagine, without speaking to me,
Made me pity him all the more."

We spoke as far as the first place
Upon the crag, which led to the next valley
Down to the bottom, where if there had been more light
When we were over the last part
Of Malebolge, so that its inhabitants
Could show themselves to us,

Divers screams pierced me through and through,
Which for the sake of compassion,
I covered my ears with my hands.

The pain emanating was like from the hospitals
Of Valdichiana, between July and September,
Combined with all the diseases

Of Maremma and Sardinia.
And such stench arose
Like from rotting limbs.

We had descended on the furthest bank
From the long crag, still on the left hand side,
Where my vision improved

Down towards the bottom, where the ministress
Of the high Lord, with infallible Justice,
Punished forgers, by recording them here.

I do not think I have ever seen a sadder sight,
Even in Aegina with the whole population sick
(When the air was so full of pestilence,

The animals, worn down by worms,
Falling and afterwards the ancient people,
According to the poets

Were restored from the seeds of ants again,)
Than what I saw through the dark valley
With the spirits languishing in divers heaps.

One lay on his belly on the back

One of the other lay, and others crawling
Shifted themselves along the dismal road.

We step by step went onward without speech,
Gazing upon and listening to the sick

Who had not strength enough to lift their bodies.

I saw two sitting leaned against each other,
As leans in heating platter against platter,
From head to foot bespotted o'er with scabs;

And never saw I plied a currycomb
By stable-boy for whom his master waits,

Or him who keeps awake unwillingly,

As every one was plying fast the bite
Of nails upon himself, for the great rage
Of itching which no other succour had.

And the nails downward with them dragged the scab,
In fashion as a knife the scales of bream,
Or any other fish that has them largest.

"O thou, that with thy fingers dost dismail thee,"
Began my Leader unto one of them,
"And makest of them pincers now and then,

Tell me if any Latian is with those
Who are herein; so may thy nails suffice thee
To all eternity unto this work."

"Latians are we, whom thou so wasted seest,
Both of us here," one weeping made reply;
"But who art thou, that questionest about us?"

And said the Guide: "One am I who descends
Down with this living man from cliff to cliff,
And I intend to show Hell unto him."

Then broken was their mutual support,
And trembling each one turned himself to me,
With others who had heard him by rebound.

Wholly to me did the good Master gather,
Saying: "Say unto them whate'er thou wishest."
And I began, since he would have it so:

Of another, and others were crawling,
Shifting themselves along the dismal road.

We went onward, step-by-step, without talking,
Gazing on and listening to the sick,

Who did not have enough strength to lift their
bodies.

I saw two sitting leaned against each other,
Like two plates stacked on top of the other,
Covered in scabs from head to foot;

And I never say a stable boy,
Who is being waited for by his master, used a
curry comb as quickly,
Or one who cannot sleep, fidget as much,

As everyone was biting and
Scratching himself, because of the great rage
Of itching, which they had no other way to
scratch.
The nails dragged the scabs downward,
Like a knife scaling a bream
Or any other large fish.

"Oh you, that destroys himself with his fingers,"
My Leader began to one of them,
"Making them pinchers now and then,

Tell me if there are any Latians
Here; So your nails may suffice you
To all eternity to this work."

"We are Latians who you wanted to see,
Both of us here," the weeping one replied;
"But who are you that questions us?"

And the Guide said: "I am the one who descends
Down with this living man from cliff to cliff,
Intending to show him Hell."

Then they broke apart
And each one turned towards me trembling,
While others who had heard him

Gathered around me, and the Master
Said: "Say whatever you wish."
So, I began like he wanted:

<table>
<tr><td>

"So may your memory not steal away
In the first world from out the minds of men,
But so may it survive 'neath many suns,

Say to me who ye are, and of what people;
Let not your foul and loathsome punishment
Make you afraid to show yourselves to me."
"I of Arezzo was," one made reply,
"And Albert of Siena had me burned;
But what I died for does not bring me here.

'Tis true I said to him, speaking in jest,
That I could rise by flight into the air,
And he who had conceit, but little wit,

Would have me show to him the art; and only
Because no Daedalus I made him, made me
Be burned by one who held him as his son.

But unto the last Bolgia of the ten,
For alchemy, which in the world I practised,
Minos, who cannot err, has me condemned."

And to the Poet said I: "Now was ever
So vain a people as the Sienese?
Not for a certainty the French by far."

Whereat the other leper, who had heard me,
Replied unto my speech: "Taking out Stricca,
Who knew the art of moderate expenses,

And Niccolo, who the luxurious use
Of cloves discovered earliest of all
Within that garden where such seed takes root;

And taking out the band, among whom squandered
Caccia d'Ascian his vineyards and vast woods,

And where his wit the Abbagliato proffered!

But, that thou know who thus doth second thee
Against the Sienese, make sharp thine eye
Tow'rds me, so that my face well answer thee,

And thou shalt see I am Capocchio's shade,
Who metals falsified by alchemy;
Thou must remember, if I well descry thee,

</td><td>

"So your memory may not fall short
From the first world,
So that it may survive many years,

Tell me who you are, and to whom you belong;
Don't let your foul and loathsome punishment
Make you afraid to show yourselves to me."
"I was of Arezzo," one began,
"And Alber of Siena had me burned;
But what I died for does not bring me here.

It is true, I told him, speaking playfully,
That I could rise into the air,
And he, who was very conceited and dim-witted,

Wanted me to show him the art, and only
Because I could not make him Daedalus,
He had me burned by his father.

But I am here in the last of the ten Bolgias,
For alchemy, which I practiced in the world,
And for which, Minos condemned me."

I turned to the Poet and said: "Was there ever
A people as vain as the Sienese?
Not even the French."

Then the other leper, who had heard me,
Replied: "Taking out Stricca,
Replied: "Taking out Stricca,

And Niccolo, who discovered
The first luxurious use of cloves,
In the garden where such seed takes root;

And taking out the band, among whom
Caccia d'Ascian squandered his vineyards and
vast woods,
And where the Abbagliato proffered from his wit!

But, so you know who feels the same as you
Against the Sienese, look carefully
At me, so you will know my face,

And you will see I am the spirit of Capocchio,
Who falsified metals by alchemy;
You must remember, if I describe myself well,

</td></tr>
</table>

How I a skilful ape of nature was."   *What a skillful ape of nature I was."*

Inferno: Canto XXX

'Twas at the time when Juno was enraged,
For Semele, against the Theban blood,
As she already more than once had shown,

So reft of reason Athamas became,
That, seeing his own wife with children twain
Walking encumbered upon either hand,

He cried: "Spread out the nets, that I may take
The lioness and her whelps upon the passage;"
And then extended his unpitying claws,

Seizing the first, who had the name Learchus,
And whirled him round, and dashed him on a rock;

And she, with the other burthen, drowned herself;--

And at the time when fortune downward hurled
The Trojan's arrogance, that all things dared,
So that the king was with his kingdom crushed,

Hecuba sad, disconsolate, and captive,
When lifeless she beheld Polyxena,
And of her Polydorus on the shore

Of ocean was the dolorous one aware,
Out of her senses like a dog she barked,
So much the anguish had her mind distorted;

But not of Thebes the furies nor the Trojan
Were ever seen in any one so cruel
In goading beasts, and much more human members,

As I beheld two shadows pale and naked,
Who, biting, in the manner ran along
That a boar does, when from the sty turned loose.

One to Capocchio came, and by the nape
Seized with its teeth his neck, so that in dragging
It made his belly grate the solid bottom.

And the Aretine, who trembling had remained,

At the time when Juno was so enraged,
For Semele, against the Theban blood,
As she had already shown more than once,

Was without reason, as Athamas came,
Seeing his own wife with two children
At each hand, slowly walking,

He cried: "Spread out the nets, so I may take
The lioness and her cubs on the passage;"
Then he extended his unpitying claws,

Seizing the first, named Learchus,
And whirled him round, and dashed him on a rock;
So, she drowned herself and the other child;

And at the time when fortune hurled downward
The Trojan's arrogance, so that all things dared,
The king was crushed with his kingdom,

And when sad Hecuba, held captive,
Held the lifeless Polyxena,
With her Polydorus on the shore

Of the ocean, became aware,
Barked like a dog, out of her senses,
Her mind lost with the amount of anguish;

But not the furies of Thebes nor the Trojans
Were ever as cruel
In goading beasts or humans

As those I saw in the shadows, pale and naked,
Who ran along, biting,
Like a boar, when turned loose from the sty.

One came to Capocchio and seized his neck
With its teeth, so in dragging him,
His belly scraped the solid bottom.

And the trembling Aretine, who remained,

Said to me: "That mad sprite is Gianni Schicchi,
And raving goes thus harrying other people."

"O," said I to him, "so may not the other
Set teeth on thee, let it not weary thee
To tell us who it is, ere it dart hence."

And he to me: "That is the ancient ghost
Of the nefarious Myrrha, who became
Beyond all rightful love her father's lover.

She came to sin with him after this manner,
By counterfeiting of another's form;
As he who goeth yonder undertook,

That he might gain the lady of the herd,
To counterfeit in himself Buoso Donati,
Making a will and giving it due form."

And after the two maniacs had passed
On whom I held mine eye, I turned it back
To look upon the other evil-born.

I saw one made in fashion of a lute,
If he had only had the groin cut off
Just at the point at which a man is forked.

The heavy dropsy, that so disproportions
The limbs with humours, which it ill concocts,
That the face corresponds not to the belly,

Compelled him so to hold his lips apart
As does the hectic, who because of thirst
One tow'rds the chin, the other upward turns.

"O ye, who without any torment are,
And why I know not, in the world of woe,"

He said to us, "behold, and be attentive

Unto the misery of Master Adam;
I had while living much of what I wished,
And now, alas! a drop of water crave.

The rivulets, that from the verdant hills
Of Cassentin descend down into Arno,
Making their channels to be cold and moist,

Said: "That mad sprite is Gianni Schicchi,
Who is so crazed he goes about harrying other
people."
"Oh," I said to him, "So the other will not
Set his teeth on you, quickly
Tell us who is here."

And he responded: "That is the ancient ghost
Of the nefarious Myrrha, who became
Her father's lover.

She came to sin with him,
By disguising herself;
As that one who goes over there,

Did to gain the lady of the herd,
By disguising himself as Buoso Donati,
And making a will."

After the two maniacs had passed
On whom I was looking, I turned back
To look at the other evil-born.

I saw one who looked like a lute,
Who had the groin cut off
At the point where a man is forked.

The heavy dropsy, that makes the limbs look
Disproportionate and humorous,
So the face does not correspond to the belly,

Compelled him to hold his lips apart
Like a heretic, who because of thirst
Turns one towards the chin and the other
upwards.
"Oh you, who are without any torment,
And who I don't know why you are in the world of
woe,"
He said to us, "Look and be attentive

To the misery of Master Adam;
While I was living, I had much of what I wished,
And now, look! I crave a drop of water.

The rivulets, that run from the verdant hills
Of Cassentin, descending down into Arno,
Which make their channels cold and moist,

Ever before me stand, and not in vain;
For far more doth their image dry me up
Than the disease which strips my face of flesh.

The rigid justice that chastises me
Draweth occasion from the place in which
I sinned, to put the more my sighs in flight.

There is Romena, where I counterfeited
The currency imprinted with the Baptist,
For which I left my body burned above.

But if I here could see the tristful soul
Of Guido, or Alessandro, or their brother,
For Branda's fount I would not give the sight.

One is within already, if the raving
Shades that are going round about speak truth;
But what avails it me, whose limbs are tied?

If I were only still so light, that in
A hundred years I could advance one inch,
I had already started on the way,

Seeking him out among this squalid folk,
Although the circuit be eleven miles,
And be not less than half a mile across.

For them am I in such a family;
They did induce me into coining florins,

Which had three carats of impurity."

And I to him: "Who are the two poor wretches
That smoke like unto a wet hand in winter,
Lying there close upon thy right-hand confines?"

"I found them here," replied he, "when I rained
Into this chasm, and since they have not turned,

Nor do I think they will for evermore.

One the false woman is who accused Joseph,
The other the false Sinon, Greek of Troy;
From acute fever they send forth such reek."

And one of them, who felt himself annoyed
At being, peradventure, named so darkly,

Stand forever before me, but not in vain;
For their image dries me up more
Than the disease that strips the flesh from my face.

The rigid justice that chastises me
Comes from the place where
I sinned, to put my sighs in place.

In Romena, I counterfeited
The currency imprinted with the Baptist,
Which caused me to leave my body burned above.

But if I could see the souls
Of Guido, Alessandro, or their brother,
I would give up all the water in Branda's fountain.

One is here already, if the raving
Spirits that go around speak truly;
But what does it matter to me, with my tied limbs?

If I were light enough, so in
A hundred years I could move one inch,
I would already be on the way

To seek him out among this squalid folk,
Although around the path may be eleven miles,
And across is not less than a half.

For with them, I am in family;
They being the ones who introduced me to coining
florins,
Which had three carats of impurity."

I asked him: "Who are the two poor wretches
That smoke like a wet hand in the winter,
Lying confined on your right side?"

"I found them here," he replied, "when I came
Into this chasm, they were like this, and they
haven't turned,
Nor do I think they ever will.

One is the false woman who accused Joseph,
The other is the liar Sinon, Greek of Troy;
They reek from an acute fever."

And one of them, who felt annoyed
At being named and named so darkly,

Smote with the fist upon his hardened paunch.

It gave a sound, as if it were a drum;
And Master Adam smote him in the face,
With arm that did not seem to be less hard,

Saying to him: "Although be taken from me
All motion, for my limbs that heavy are,
I have an arm unfettered for such need."

Whereat he answer made: "When thou didst go
Unto the fire, thou hadst it not so ready:
But hadst it so and more when thou wast coining."

The dropsical: "Thou sayest true in that;
But thou wast not so true a witness there,
Where thou wast questioned of the truth at Troy."

"If I spake false, thou falsifiedst the coin,"
Said Sinon; "and for one fault I am here,
And thou for more than any other demon."

"Remember, perjurer, about the horse,"
He made reply who had the swollen belly,
"And rueful be it thee the whole world knows it."

"Rueful to thee the thirst be wherewith cracks
Thy tongue," the Greek said, "and the putrid water
That hedges so thy paunch before thine eyes."

Then the false-coiner: "So is gaping wide
Thy mouth for speaking evil, as 'tis wont;
Because if I have thirst, and humour stuff me

Thou hast the burning and the head that aches,
And to lick up the mirror of Narcissus
Thou wouldst not want words many to invite thee."

In listening to them was I wholly fixed
When said the Master to me: "Now just look,
For little wants it that I quarrel with thee."

When him I heard in anger speak to me,
I turned me round towards him with such shame
That still it eddies through my memory.

And as he is who dreams of his own harm,
Who dreaming wishes it may be a dream,

Hit himself with his fist on his hardened paunch.

It gave a sound, as if it were a drum;
And Master Adam hit him in the face,
With his own hardened arm,

Saying: "Although motion has been taken from me
Because my limbs are too heavy,
I have one arm that can be used, if the need arises."
The other answered: "When you went
In the fire, you did not have it so ready,
As you did when you were coining."

Master Adam said: "What you say is true,
But you were not such a true witness,
When you were questioned at Troy."

"If I spoke falsely, you falsified the coin,"
Sinon said; "And for one fault I am here,
And you are here for many."

"Remember, perjurer, about the horse,"
The one with the swollen belly replied,
"And you should be rueful that the whole world knows it."
"You be rueful where the thirst has cracked
Your tongue," the Greek said, "And the putrid
Water that hedges you must look upon."

Then the false coiner returned: "Like your gaping
Mouth is for speaking evil,
Because if I have thirst, and humor me here

You are burning and have a head that aches,
And to like the mirror of Narcissus
You wouldn't lack for words."

In listening to them, I was completely transfixed,
When my Master said: "Now look,
I don't want to quarrel with you."

When I heard him speak in anger to me,
I turned around with such shame
That it still eddies in my memory.

And like one who dreams of his own harm,
Who wishes it to be a dream,

So that he craves what is, as if it were not;

Such I became, not having power to speak,
For to excuse myself I wished, and still
Excused myself, and did not think I did it.

"Less shame doth wash away a greater fault,"
The Master said, "than this of thine has been;
Therefore thyself disburden of all sadness,

And make account that I am aye beside thee,
If e'er it come to pass that fortune bring thee
Where there are people in a like dispute;

For a base wish it is to wish to hear it."

So he craves what is, as if it were not,

I became such, not having power to speak,
To excuse myself,
Even though I excused myself, and did not think I did.
"Less shame washes away greater fault,"
The Master said, "Than this of yours has been;
Therefore, do not be burdened by sadness,

And make note that I am with you.
If fortune ever brings you
Where people are disputing;

It is a base wish to wish to hear it."

Inferno: Canto XXXI

One and the selfsame tongue first wounded me,
So that it tinged the one cheek and the other,
And then held out to me the medicine;

Thus do I hear that once Achilles' spear,
His and his father's, used to be the cause
First of a sad and then a gracious boon.

We turned our backs upon the wretched valley,
Upon the bank that girds it round about,
Going across it without any speech.

There it was less than night, and less than day,
So that my sight went little in advance;
But I could hear the blare of a loud horn,

So loud it would have made each thunder faint,
Which, counter to it following its way,
Mine eyes directed wholly to one place.

After the dolorous discomfiture
When Charlemagne the holy emprise lost,
So terribly Orlando sounded not.

Short while my head turned thitherward I held
When many lofty towers I seemed to see,
Whereat I: "Master, say, what town is this?"

And he to me: "Because thou peerest forth
Athwart the darkness at too great a distance,
It happens that thou errest in thy fancy.

Well shalt thou see, if thou arrivest there,
How much the sense deceives itself by distance;
Therefore a little faster spur thee on."

Then tenderly he took me by the hand,
And said: "Before we farther have advanced,
That the reality may seem to thee

Less strange, know that these are not towers, but giants,
And they are in the well, around the bank,

The same tongue that first wounded me,
Reddened the one cheek then the other,
And then gave me more medicine,

Like when I heard that once Achilles's spear,
Which also belonged to his father, was the cause
Of sadness and then graciousness.

We turned our backs upon the wretched valley,
On the bank that goes around,
Without speaking.

There it was neither night nor day,
So I could not see very far;
But I could hear the blare of a loud horn,

So loud, it would have made thunder faint.
While following the sound,
My eyes were directed to one place.

After the sad time,
When Charlemagne lost the holy empire,
Orlando remained silent.

After a short while I turned my head
And saw many lofty towers.
Then I said: "Master, tell me, what town is this?"

And he replied: "Because you are looking
Through the darkness at a great distance,
Your imagination is wrong.

You will see well, when you arrive there,
How much distance can deceive you;
Therefore, let's go a little faster."

Then he took my hand tenderly,
And said: "Before we go further,
So what you see is not a surprise

Know that the towers you see are giants.
They are in the well around the bank,

From navel downward, one and all of them."

As, when the fog is vanishing away,
Little by little doth the sight refigure
Whate'er the mist that crowds the air conceals,

So, piercing through the dense and darksome air,
More and more near approaching tow'rd the verge,
My error fled, and fear came over me;

Because as on its circular parapets

Montereggione crowns itself with towers,
E'en thus the margin which surrounds the well

With one half of their bodies turreted
The horrible giants, whom Jove menaces
E'en now from out the heavens when he thunders.

And I of one already saw the face,
Shoulders, and breast, and great part of the belly,
And down along his sides both of the arms.

Certainly Nature, when she left the making
Of animals like these, did well indeed,
By taking such executors from Mars;

And if of elephants and whales she doth not

Repent her, whosoever looketh subtly
More just and more discreet will hold her for it;

For where the argument of intellect
Is added unto evil will and power,
No rampart can the people make against it.

His face appeared to me as long and large
As is at Rome the pine-cone of Saint Peter's,
And in proportion were the other bones;

So that the margin, which an apron was
Down from the middle, showed so much of him
Above it, that to reach up to his hair

Three Frieslanders in vain had vaunted them;
For I beheld thirty great palms of him
Down from the place where man his mantle buckles.

Hidden from the navel down."

Like when the fog vanishes away,
Little by little the sight became clearer
And whatever was concealed by the mist

Pierced through the dense and darksome air,
The closer we approached,
As my error was corrected and fear overtook me;

Because as Montereggione crowns itself with
towers
On circular parapets,
Surrounding the margins of the well

With one half of their bodies buried
Stood the horrible giants, whom Jove menaces
Even now from out of heaven when he thunders.

I already saw the face,
Shoulders, breast, and great belly of one,
And down along his sides laid both of his arms.

Certainly Nature, when she finished making
Animals like these, did well indeed,
By taking such advice from Mars.

And if she did not repent when she made elephants
and whales,
Whoever looked subtly
Would hold her responsible for it;

For where slight intelligence
Is added to evil will and power,
People do not have a chance against it.

His face appeared to me as long and large
As the Roman pine tree of Saint Peter's,
And in proportion with his other bones;

So that the margin, which was an apron
Down the middle, showed so much of him
Above it, that to reach up to his hair

Three Frieslanders had tried and failed;
I saw thirty great palms of him
Down from the place where man buckles his
mantle.

"Raphael mai amech izabi almi,"
Began to clamour the ferocious mouth,
To which were not befitting sweeter psalms.

And unto him my Guide: "Soul idiotic,
Keep to thy horn, and vent thyself with that,
When wrath or other passion touches thee.

Search round thy neck, and thou wilt find the belt
Which keeps it fastened, O bewildered soul,
And see it, where it bars thy mighty breast."

Then said to me: "He doth himself accuse;
This one is Nimrod, by whose evil thought
One language in the world is not still used.

Here let us leave him and not speak in vain;
For even such to him is every language
As his to others, which to none is known."

Therefore a longer journey did we make,
Turned to the left, and a crossbow-shot oft
We found another far more fierce and large.

In binding him, who might the master be

I cannot say; but he had pinioned close
Behind the right arm, and in front the other,

With chains, that held him so begirt about
From the neck down, that on the part uncovered
It wound itself as far as the fifth gyre.

"This proud one wished to make experiment
Of his own power against the Supreme Jove,"
My Leader said, "whence he has such a guerdon.

Ephialtes is his name; he showed great prowess.
What time the giants terrified the gods;
The arms he wielded never more he moves."

And I to him: "If possible, I should wish
That of the measureless Briareus
These eyes of mine might have experience."

Whence he replied: "Thou shalt behold Antaeus
Close by here, who can speak and is unbound
Who at the bottom of all crime shall place us.

"Raphael mai amech izabi almi,"
The ferocious mouth began to clamor,
With sweet psalms.

My guide replied: "Idiotic soul,
Keep to your horn and vent yourself with that,
When you are overcome with wrath or some other
passion.
Search around your neck and you will find the belt
Which holds it, oh bewildered soul,
And see where it rests on your chest."

Then he said to me: "He does accuse himself;
This one is Nimrod, by whose evil thought
One language in the world is still not
accustomed."
Here let us leave him and not speak badly
Even though all language to him is bad
As his language is to others

Therefore, we made a longer journey,
Turned left and took off,
Finding another far more fierce and large giant.

In binding him, I cannot say who the master might
be;
But he was pinned underneath the right arm
And in the front

Chains were fastened around him
Winding from the neck down
As far as the fifty gyre.

"This proud one wished to experiment
With his own power against the supreme Jove,"
My Leader said, "So this is his punishment.

Ephialtes is his name; he showed great prowess.
In the time when the giants terrified the gods;
He wielded his arms and now he never moves."

I said: "If possible, I would like to
See the measureless Briareus
With these eyes of mine."

He replied: "You will see Antaeus
Who is close by here, can speak, and is unbound;
He will place us at the bottom of this crime pit.

Much farther yon is he whom thou wouldst see,
And he is bound, and fashioned like to this one,
Save that he seems in aspect more ferocious."

There never was an earthquake of such might
That it could shake a tower so violently,
As Ephialtes suddenly shook himself.

Then was I more afraid of death than ever,
For nothing more was needful than the fear,
If I had not beheld the manacles.

Then we proceeded farther in advance,
And to Antaeus came, who, full five ells
Without the head, forth issued from the cavern.

"O thou, who in the valley fortunate,
Which Scipio the heir of glory made,
When Hannibal turned back with all his hosts,

Once brought'st a thousand lions for thy prey,
And who, hadst thou been at the mighty war

Among thy brothers, some it seems still think

The sons of Earth the victory would have gained:
Place us below, nor be disdainful of it,
There where the cold doth lock Cocytus up.

Make us not go to Tityus nor Typhoeus;
This one can give of that which here is longed for;
Therefore stoop down, and do not curl thy lip.

Still in the world can he restore thy fame;
Because he lives, and still expects long life,
If to itself Grace call him not untimely."

So said the Master; and in haste the other
His hands extended and took up my Guide,--

Hands whose great pressure Hercules once felt.

Virgilius, when he felt himself embraced,
Said unto me: "Draw nigh, that I may take thee;"
Then of himself and me one bundle made.

---

*The one you will see is much farther over there,
He is bound and fashioned like this one,
And seems more ferocious."*

*There was never an earthquake of such might
That could shake a tower so violently,
As Ephialtes shook himself at that moment.*

*He made me more afraid of death than ever,
Needing nothing other than the feel of fear,
With him being held by manacles.*

*Then we proceeded farther,
And came to Antaeus who was about 25 feet
Without the head.*

*"Oh you, who in the fortunate valley,
Which Scipio the heir made of glory
When Hannibal turned back with all his hosts*

*Once brought a thousand lions for your prey,
And who, had you been at the mighty war with
your brothers,
Some still think*

*Would have been victorious,
Place us below, and don't be disdainful of it,
Where the cold locks up Cocytus.*

*Do not make us go to Tityus or Typhoeus;
This one can give you what you long for;
So stop down, and do not curl up your lip.*

*He can still restore your fame up in the world;
Because he lives, and expects to continue living,
If Grace does not call him."*

*The Master said; and in haste the other
Extended his hands, whose pressure Hercules
once felt,
And took up my Guide,*

*Virgilius, who feeling himself embraced,
Said to me: "Come here, so I may take you,"
Then he made a bundle of us both.*

As seems the Carisenda, to behold

Beneath the leaning side, when goes a cloud
Above it so that opposite it hangs;

Such did Antaeus seem to me, who stood
Watching to see him stoop, and then it was
I could have wished to go some other way.

But lightly in the abyss, which swallows up
Judas with Lucifer, he put us down;
Nor thus bowed downward made he there delay,

But, as a mast does in a ship, uprose.

Like the Carisenda, seeing beneath the leaning side,
When a cloud goes
Above it so that it hangs opposite;

Antaeus seemed to me,
When I watched him stoop,
Wishing I could go some other way.

But lightly in the abyss, which swallows up
Judas with Lucifer, he put us down;
Bowing downward, he made a delay,

But like a mast does in a ship, he up rose.

Inferno: Canto XXXII

If I had rhymes both rough and stridulous,
As were appropriate to the dismal hole
Down upon which thrust all the other rocks,

I would press out the juice of my conception
More fully; but because I have them not,
Not without fear I bring myself to speak;

For 'tis no enterprise to take in jest,
To sketch the bottom of all the universe,
Nor for a tongue that cries Mamma and Babbo.

But may those Ladies help this verse of mine,
Who helped Amphion in enclosing Thebes,
That from the fact the word be not diverse.

O rabble ill-begotten above all,
Who're in the place to speak of which is hard,
'Twere better ye had here been sheep or goats!

When we were down within the darksome well,
Beneath the giant's feet, but lower far,
And I was scanning still the lofty wall,

I heard it said to me: "Look how thou steppest!
Take heed thou do not trample with thy feet
The heads of the tired, miserable brothers!"

Whereat I turned me round, and saw before me
And underfoot a lake, that from the frost
The semblance had of glass, and not of water.

So thick a veil ne'er made upon its current
In winter-time Danube in Austria,
Nor there beneath the frigid sky the Don,

As there was here; so that if Tambernich
Had fallen upon it, or Pietrapana,
E'en at the edge 'twould not have given a creak.

And as to croak the frog doth place himself

If I had rough ridiculous rhymes,
Appropriate to the dismal hole,
Down on which thrust all the other rocks,

I would press out what I conceived
More fully; but because I do not have them,
I bring myself with fear to speak;

For it's no enterprise to take in jest,
To sketch the bottom of the universe,
Or for the tongue of a child.

But may the Ladies help me with this verse,
Like they helped Amphion in enclosing Thebes,
So, I may stay true to the facts.

Oh, ill-begotten rabble above all,
Who're in the place where it is hard to speak,
It would be better if you were sheep or goats!

When we were down within the dark well,
A little lower, beneath the giant's feet,
I was scanning the lofty wall,

And I heard it said to me: "Look where you step!
Do not trample with your feet
The heads of the tired, miserable brothers!"

I turned around and saw before me,
A lake under my feet that from the frost
Resembled glass, not water.

There has never been a current as thick on
The Danube in Austria during the winter,
Nor there beneath the frigid sky of Don,

As there was here; So if Tambernich
Had fallen on it or Pietrapana,
Even at the edge, it would not have given a creak.

And as the croaking frog places himself

With muzzle out of water,--when is dreaming	*With his head out of the water,--while he's dreaming*
Of gleaning oftentimes the peasant-girl,--	*Of gleaning the peasant-girl,--*
Livid, as far down as where shame appears, Were the disconsolate shades within the ice, Setting their teeth unto the note of storks.	*Livid, as far down as where shame appears, Were the disconsolate shades within the ice, Setting there chattering teeth to the notes of storks.*
Each one his countenance held downward bent; From mouth the cold, from eyes the doleful heart Among them witness of itself procures.	*Each one's countenance was bent downward; I was a witness among them and saw, The cold pour forth from the mouth and from the eyes the doleful heart.*
When round about me somewhat I had looked, I downward turned me, and saw two so close, The hair upon their heads together mingled.	*When I had looked around somewhat, I turned down and saw two so close, The hair on their heads mingled together.*
"Ye who so strain your breasts together, tell me," I said, "who are you;" and they bent their necks, And when to me their faces they had lifted,	*"You who strain your breasts together, tell me," I said, "Who you are;" and they bent their necks, And when they lifted their faces towards me,*
Their eyes, which first were only moist within, Gushed o'er the eyelids, and the frost congealed The tears between, and locked them up again.	*Their eyes, which were only moist at first, Gushed over the eyelids, and the frost froze The tears between, and locked them up again.*
Clamp never bound together wood with wood So strongly; whereat they, like two he-goats, Butted together, so much wrath o'ercame them.	*A clamp never bound wood to wood together So strongly; whereat they, like two male goats, Butted together, so much wrath came over them.*
And one, who had by reason of the cold Lost both his ears, still with his visage downward, Said: "Why dost thou so mirror thyself in us?	*And one, who had lost both his ears Due to the cold, with his face downward, Said: "Why are you so interested in us?*
If thou desire to know who these two are, The valley whence Bisenzio descends Belonged to them and to their father Albert	*If you desire to know who these two are, The valley from where Bisenzio descends Belonged to them and their father Albert.*
They from one body came, and all Caina Thou shalt search through, and shalt not find a shade More worthy to be fixed in gelatine;	*They came from one body, and you can search Through all of Caina, and not find a spirit More worthy to be fixed in gelatin;*
Not he in whom were broken breast and shadow At one and the same blow by Arthur's hand; Focaccia not; not he who me encumbers	*Not he, in whom were broken breast and shadow At one and the same blow by Arthur's hand; Not me, nor Focaccia, nor even the one who is in front of me*
So with his head I see no farther forward, And bore the name of Sassol Mascheroni; Well knowest thou who he was, if thou art Tuscan.	*So I cannot see farther due to his head, Who bore the name of Sassol Mascheroni; You would know him well, if you were Tuscan.*

And that thou put me not to further speech, Know that I Camicion de' Pazzi was, And wait Carlino to exonerate me."	*And just so you know,* *I was Camicion de' Pazzi,* *Who waited for Carlino to exonerate me."*
Then I beheld a thousand faces, made Purple with cold; whence o'er me comes a shudder And evermore will come, at frozen ponds.	*Then I saw a thousand faces, made* *Purple with cold; when a shudder came over me,* *Like comes over you at frozen ponds.*
And while we were advancing tow'rds the middle, Where everything of weight unites together, And I was shivering in the eternal shade,	*While we were advancing towards the middle,* *Where everything of weight unites together,* *And I was shivering from the eternal dark,*
Whether 'twere will, or destiny, or chance, I know not; but in walking 'mong the heads I struck my foot hard in the face of one.	*Whether it were will, destiny, or chance,* *I don't know; but in walking among the heads* *I struck my foot hard on the face of one.*
Weeping he growled: "Why dost thou trample me?	*Weeping, he growled: "Why do you trample on* *me?*
Unless thou comest to increase the vengeance	*Unless you come to increase the vengeance of* *Montaperti,*
of Montaperti, why dost thou molest me?"	*Why do you strike me?"*
And I: "My Master, now wait here for me, That I through him may issue from a doubt; Then thou mayst hurry me, as thou shalt wish."	*And I: "My Master, now wait for me here,* *That I may speak with him;* *Then you may hurry me, as you wish."*
The Leader stopped; and to that one I said Who was blaspheming vehemently still: "Who art thou, that thus reprehendest others?"	*The Leader stopped; and I spoke to that one* *Who was blaspheming so vehemently:* *"Who are you, that hates others?"*
"Now who art thou, that goest through Antenora Smiting," replied he, "other people's cheeks, So that, if thou wert living, 'twere too much?"	*"Now who are you, that goes through Antenora* *Smiting," he replied, "Other people's cheeks,* *So that, if you were living, it would be too much?"*
"Living I am, and dear to thee it may be,	*"I am living, and my response may be dear to* *you,"*
Was my response, "if thou demandest fame, That 'mid the other notes thy name I place."	*I responded, "If you demand fame,* *That amidst the other living I may place your* *name."*
And he to me: "For the reverse I long; Take thyself hence, and give me no more trouble; For ill thou knowest to flatter in this hollow."	*To which he replied: "I long for the reverse;* *Go away and give me no more trouble;* *For it will do you no good to flatter in this place."*
Then by the scalp behind I seized upon him, And said: "It must needs be thou name thyself, Or not a hair remain upon thee here."	*Then I seized his scalp from behind,* *And said: "You must give up your name,* *Or not a hair will remain on your head."*
Whence he to me: "Though thou strip off my hair,	*"Though you strip off my hair,*

I will not tell thee who I am, nor show thee,
If on my head a thousand times thou fall."

I had his hair in hand already twisted,
And more than one shock of it had pulled out,
He barking, with his eyes held firmly down,

When cried another: "What doth ail thee, Bocca?
Is't not enough to clatter with thy jaws,
But thou must bark? what devil touches thee?"

"Now," said I, "I care not to have thee speak,
Accursed traitor; for unto thy shame
I will report of thee veracious news."

"Begone," replied he, "and tell what thou wilt,
But be not silent, if thou issue hence,
Of him who had just now his tongue so prompt;

He weepeth here the silver of the French;
'I saw,' thus canst thou phrase it, 'him of Duera
There where the sinners stand out in the cold.'

If thou shouldst questioned be who else was there,

Thou hast beside thee him of Beccaria
Of whom the gorget Florence slit asunder;

Gianni del Soldanier, I think, may be
Yonder with Ganellon, and Tebaldello
Who oped Faenza when the people slep."

Already we had gone away from him,
When I beheld two frozen in one hole,
So that one head a hood was to the other;

And even as bread through hunger is devoured,
The uppermost on the other set his teeth,
There where the brain is to the nape united.

Not in another fashion Tydeus gnawed
The temples of Menalippus in disdain,
Than that one did the skull and the other things.

"O thou, who showest by such bestial sign
Thy hatred against him whom thou art eating,
Tell me the wherefore," said I, "with this compact,

I will not tell you who I am, or show you
If you fall on my head a thousand times."

I had his hair twisted in my hand,
Pulling out more than one shock,
While he barked, with his eyes held firmly down,

When another cried: "What ails you, Bocca?
Isn't it enough to clatter with your jaws,
But you must bark? What devil touches you?"

"Now," I said, "I don't care to speak to you,
Accursed traitor; for shame on you
I will report your veracious news."

"Be gone," he said, "and say what you will,
But don't be silent, if you leave here,
Of him who just opened his mouth;

He wept here the silver of the French;
'I saw,' but cannot phrase it, 'he of Duera
There where the sinners stand out in the cold.'

If you should be questioned about who else was
here,
You should know you are beside him of Beccaria,
Who was slit asunder by the gorget of Florence;

Gianni del Soldanier, I think, may be
Over there with Ganellon and Tebaldello
Who destroyed Faenza while the people slept."

We had already gone away from him,
When I saw two frozen in one hole,
So that one's head was a hood to the other;

And like bread is devoured with hunger,
The uppermost spirit set his teeth on the other
Where the brain is connected to the neck.

Like Tydeus gnawed
The temples of Menalippus in disdain,
The one chewed at the skull of the other.

"Oh you, who show by bestiality
Your hatred against him you are eating,
Tell me why," I said, "And I promise,

That if thou rightfully of him complain,

In knowing who ye are, and his transgression,
I in the world above repay thee for it,

If that wherewith I speak be not dried up."

That if you rightfully speak truthfully of his identity
And transgression, in knowing who you are,
I will repay you in the world above for it,

If what I speak does not dry up."

Inferno: Canto XXXIII

His mouth uplifted from his grim repast,
That sinner, wiping it upon the hair
Of the same head that he behind had wasted.

His mouth uplifted from his grim pastime,
Wiping it upon the hair
Of the same head that he had wasted behind.

Then he began: "Thou wilt that I renew
The desperate grief, which wrings my heart already

Then he began: "You will that I renew
The desperate grief, which already wrings my
heart

To think of only, ere I speak of it;

To only think of it, with speaking;

But if my words be seed that may bear fruit
Of infamy to the traitor whom I gnaw,
Speaking and weeping shalt thou see together.

But if my words that bear fruit
Of infamy to the traitor whom I gnaw,
You will see both speaking and weeping.

I know not who thou art, nor by what mode
Thou hast come down here; but a Florentine
Thou seemest to me truly, when I hear thee.

I don't know who you are, or how
You came down here; but a Florentine
Is what you seem to me, when I hear you speak.

Thou hast to know I was Count Ugolino,
And this one was Ruggieri the Archbishop;
Now I will tell thee why I am such a neighbour.

You must know I was Count Ugolino,
And this one was Ruggieri the Archbishop;
Now I will tell you why I am such a neighbor.

That, by effect of his malicious thoughts,
Trusting in him I was made prisoner,
And after put to death, I need not say;

By his malicious thoughts,
I trusted him and was made a prisoner,
And needless to say, I was put to death.

But ne'ertheless what thou canst not have heard,
That is to say, how cruel was my death,
Hear shalt thou, and shalt know if he has wronged me.

Nevertheless what you need to hear
Is how cruel my death was,
And you will hear and know he wronged me.

A narrow perforation in the mew,
Which bears because of me the title of Famine,
And in which others still must be locked up,

A narrow perforation in the cage
Called Famine, because of me,
Where others are still locked up,

Had shown me through its opening many moons
Already, when I dreamed the evil dream
Which of the future rent for me the veil.

Showed me many moons while I was there,
When I dreamed the evil dream,
Of my future which included the veil.

This one appeared to me as lord and master,
Hunting the wolf and whelps upon the mountain
For which the Pisans cannot Lucca see.

This one appeared to me as lord and master,
Hunting the wolf and pups upon the mountain,
Which blocks the Pisans from the Luccans.

With sleuth-hounds gaunt, and eager, and well trained,

With gaunt, eager, and well trained hounds,

Gualandi with Sismondi and Lanfianchi He had sent out before him to the front.	*Gualandi, Sismondi, and Lanfianchi,* *Were sent before him to the front.*
After brief course seemed unto me forespent The father and the sons, and with sharp tushes It seemed to me I saw their flanks ripped open.	*After some time had passed,* *The father and sons* *Were torn apart by their sharp teeth.*
When I before the morrow was awake, Moaning amid their sleep I heard my sons Who with me were, and asking after bread.	*Before the next morning,* *I heard my sons moaning in their sleep,* *Asking for bread.*
Cruel indeed art thou, if yet thou grieve not, Thinking of what my heart foreboded me,	*You are cruel, if you do not grieve,* *When you think of what my heart must have gone* *through,*
And weep'st thou not, what art thou wont to weep at?	*And if you don't weep at my story.*
They were awake now, and the hour drew nigh At which our food used to be brought to us, And through his dream was each one apprehensive;	*They were awake now, and the hour drew near* *When our food was brought to us,* *And through this dream each one was fearful;*
And I heard locking up the under door Of the horrible tower; whereat without a word I gazed into the faces of my sons.	*I heard the locking up of the door underneath* *Of the horrible tower, whereat without a word,* *Gazed into the faces of my sons.*
I wept not, I within so turned to stone; They wept; and darling little Anselm mine Said: 'Thou dost gaze so, father, what doth ail thee?'	*I did not weep, instead I turned to stone;* *They wept; and my darling little Anselm,* *Said: 'Why are you looking at us like that, father?'*
Still not a tear I shed, nor answer made All of that day, nor yet the night thereafter, Until another sun rose on the world.	*Still I did not shed a tear or answer them* *All day and the following night,* *Until the next morning.*
As now a little glimmer made its way Into the dolorous prison, and I saw Upon four faces my own very aspect,	*A little glimmer made its way* *Into the sullen prison, and I saw* *On four faces, my very own aspect.*
Both of my hands in agony I bit; And, thinking that I did it from desire Of eating, on a sudden they uprose,	*I bit both of my hands in agony;* *And, thinking that I did it from hunger,* *They suddenly arose,*
And said they: 'Father, much less pain 'twill give us If thou do eat of us; thyself didst clothe us With this poor flesh, and do thou strip it off.'	*And said: 'It will pain us less* *If you eat us, since you clothed us;* *With this poor flesh, fill yourself.'*
I calmed me then, not to make them more sad. That day we all were silent, and the next. Ah! obdurate earth, wherefore didst thou not open?	*I calmed then, not to make them sadder.* *That day and the next we were all silent.* *Ah, obdurate earth, why didn't you open?*

When we had come unto the fourth day, Gaddo Threw himself down outstretched before my feet, Saying, 'My father, why dost thou not help me?'	*On the fourth day, Gaddo* *Threw himself down outstretched at my feet,* *Saying, 'My father, why don't you help me?'*
And there he died; and, as thou seest me, I saw the three fall, one by one, between The fifth day and the sixth; whence I betook me,	*Then he died; And as you see me now,* *I saw the others fall, one-by-one, between* *The fifth and sixth day; when I took*
Already blind, to groping over each, And three days called them after they were dead; Then hunger did what sorrow could not do."	*From blindness, groping over each,* *And three days after they were dead;* *Hunger did what sorrow could not do."*
When he had said this, with his eyes distorted, The wretched skull resumed he with his teeth, Which, as a dog's, upon the bone were strong.	*When he had said this, with his distorted eyes,* *He resumed the wretched skull with his teeth,* *Like a dog on a strong bone.*
Ah! Pisa, thou opprobrium of the people Of the fair land there where the 'Si' doth sound, Since slow to punish thee thy neighbours are,	*Ah Pisa! You disgraceful people* *Of the fair land where the 'Si' is said,* *Since your neighbors are slow to punish you,*
Let the Capraia and Gorgona move, And make a hedge across the mouth of Arno That every person in thee it may drown!	*Let the Capraia and Gorgona move,* *And make a hedge across the mouth of Arno* *So every person may drown!*
For if Count Ugolino had the fame Of having in thy castles thee betrayed, Thou shouldst not on such cross have put his sons.	*For if Count Ugolino had the fame* *Of betraying you,* *You should not have put his sons on the cross.*
Guiltless of any crime, thou modern Thebes! Their youth made Uguccione and Brigata, And the other two my song doth name above!	*Guiltless of any crime, you modern Thebes!* *Their youth made Uguccione and Brigata,* *And the other two the name of my song above!*
We passed still farther onward, where the ice Another people ruggedly enswathes, Not downward turned, but all of them reversed.	*We passed on farther, where the ice* *Ruggedly enclosed another people,* *Turned upright.*
Weeping itself there does not let them weep, And grief that finds a barrier in the eyes Turns itself inward to increase the anguish;	*Unable to weep,* *Grief found a barrier in the eyes,* *Turning itself inward to increase the anguish;*
Because the earliest tears a cluster form, And, in the manner of a crystal visor, Fill all the cup beneath the eyebrow full.	*Because the earliest tears formed a cluster,* *And, like a crystal visor,* *Filled the eyes like a cup.*
And notwithstanding that, as in a callus, Because of cold all sensibility Its station had abandoned in my face,	*To make matters worse, like a callus,* *Because of the cold,* *All sensibilities had abandoned my face,*

Still it appeared to me I felt some wind; Whence I: "My Master, who sets this in motion?	*Still, I felt some wind;* *When I asked: "My Master, who sets this in motion?*
Is not below here every vapour quenched?"	*Isn't every vapor here quenched?"*
Whence he to me: "Full soon shalt thou be where Thine eye shall answer make to thee of this,	*He replied: "You will soon be where* *You will have the answer to who controls all of this,*
Seeing the cause which raineth down the blast."	*Seeing the cause which rains down the blast."*
And one of the wretches of the frozen crust Cried out to us: "O souls so merciless That the last post is given unto you,	*Then one of the wretches frozen in the crust* *Cried out to us: "Oh souls, so merciless* *That the last post is given to you,*
Lift from mine eyes the rigid veils, that I May vent the sorrow which impregns my heart A little, e'er the weeping recongeal."	*Lift the rigid veils from my eyes* *So I may vent the sorrow swelling in my heart,* *Where a little weeping will reseal."*
Whence I to him: "If thou wouldst have me help thee Say who thou wast; and if I free thee not, May I go to the bottom of the ice."	*I responded: "If you would help me* *Say who you were, and if I don't fee you,* *May I go to the bottom of the ice."*
Then he replied: "I am Friar Alberigo; He am I of the fruit of the bad garden, Who here a date am getting for my fig."	*He said: "I am Friar Alberigo;* *I am of the fruit of the bad garden* *Who is getting a date for his fig."*
"O," said I to him, "now art thou, too, dead?" And he to me: "How may my body fare Up in the world, no knowledge I possess.	*"Oh," I said to him, "you are dead now?"* *And he replied: "How my body is* *In the world, I don't now.*
Such an advantage has this Ptolomaea, That oftentimes the soul descendeth here Sooner than Atropos in motion sets it.	*This Ptolomaea has such an advantage,* *That often the soul descends here* *Before death is set in motion.*
And, that thou mayest more willingly remove From off my countenance these glassy tears, Know that as soon as any soul betrays	*And, so you will more willingly remove* *These glassy tears from my face,* *Know that as soon as any soul betrays*
As I have done, his body by a demon Is taken from him, who thereafter rules it, Until his time has wholly been revolved.	*As I have done, his body is taken from him,* *And a demon rules it thereafter,* *Until his time has been revolved.*
Itself down rushes into such a cistern; And still perchance above appears the body Of yonder shade, that winters here behind me.	*Then it rushes down into a cistern;* *And still, by chance the body appears above* *Like I am here.*
This thou shouldst know, if thou hast just come down;	*You should also know, if you have just come down;*

It is Ser Branca d' Oria, and many years
Have passed away since he was thus locked up."

"I think," said I to him, "thou dost deceive me;
For Branca d' Oria is not dead as yet,
And eats, and drinks, and sleeps, and puts on clothes."

"In moat above," said he, "of Malebranche,
There where is boiling the tenacious pitch,
As yet had Michel Zanche not arrived,
When this one left a devil in his stead
In his own body and one near of kin,
Who made together with him the betrayal.

But hitherward stretch out thy hand forthwith,
Open mine eyes;"--and open them I did not,
And to be rude to him was courtesy.

Ah, Genoese! ye men at variance
With every virtue, full of every vice
Wherefore are ye not scattered from the world?

For with the vilest spirit of Romagna
I found of you one such, who for his deeds
In soul already in Cocytus bathes,

And still above in body seems alive!

Ser Brana d' Oria is here, and many years
Have passed away since he was locked up."

"I think you are deceiving me," I said,
"For Branca d' Oria isn't dead yet,
He eats, drinks, sleeps, and puts on his clothes."

"In the moat above," he said, "of Malebranche,
There where the boiling pitch is,
Michel Zanche had yet to arrive,
When this one, left a devil in his place
Of his own body, and one of his relatives
Who betrayed with him.

But stretch out your hand, now,
Open my eyes;" and I did not open them,
Being rude to him.

Ah, Genoese! You varied men
Full of every virtue and vice
Why aren't you scattered from the world?

For with the vilest spirit of Romagna
I found one of you, who for his deeds
His soul already bathed in Cocytus,

Even though his body seemed to live!

Inferno: Canto XXXIV

"'Vexilla Regis prodeunt Inferni'
Towards us; therefore look in front of thee,"
My Master said, "if thou discernest him."

As, when there breathes a heavy fog, or when
Our hemisphere is darkening into night,
Appears far off a mill the wind is turning,

Methought that such a building then I saw;
And, for the wind, I drew myself behind
My Guide, because there was no other shelter.

Now was I, and with fear in verse I put it,
There where the shades were wholly covered up,
And glimmered through like unto straws in glass.

Some prone are lying, others stand erect,
This with the head, and that one with the soles;
Another, bow-like, face to feet inverts.

When in advance so far we had proceeded,
That it my Master pleased to show to me
The creature who once had the beauteous semblance,

He from before me moved and made me stop,
Saying: "Behold Dis, and behold the place
Where thou with fortitude must arm thyself."

How frozen I became and powerless then,
Ask it not, Reader, for I write it not,
Because all language would be insufficient.

I did not die, and I alive remained not;
Think for thyself now, hast thou aught of wit,
What I became, being of both deprived.

The Emperor of the kingdom dolorous
From his mid-breast forth issued from the ice;
And better with a giant I compare

Than do the giants with those arms of his;
Consider now how great must be that whole,

"'Vexilla Regis prodeunt Inferni' is
Towards us; so look in front of you,"
My Master said, "if you understand him."

Like when a heavy fog breathes, or when
Our world is darkening into night,
A mill appeared far off, turning with the wind,

I thought I saw such a building;
And, because of the wind I drew myself behind
My Guide, because there was no other shelter.

Now I was, and fearfully I put it,
Where the shades were wholly covered up,
And glimmered through like straws in glass.

Some were lying, others were standing,
Some were heads up, others were feet up,
While others were inverted like a bow, face to feet.

When we had advanced so far,
My Master was pleased to show me,
The creature, who was once beautiful.

My Master moved from in front and made me stop,
Saying: "Behold Dis, and the place
Where you must arm yourself with fortitude."

I became frozen and powerless then,
And do not ask Reader, for I can't write it,
Because no language is sufficient.

I did not die, and I did not remain alive;
Think for yourself now, if you have the mind,
What I became, being deprived of life and death.

The Emperor of the dolorous kingdom
Issued forth ice from his chest;
And I would do better to compare him with a giant

With those arms of his;
Consider now how great he must be,

Which unto such a part conforms itself.	*When a part of him was so great.*
Were he as fair once, as he now is foul, / And lifted up his brow against his Maker, / Well may proceed from him all tribulation.	*If he were once as fair as he now is foul, / And lifted up his brow against his Maker, / Tribulation may well proceed from him.*
O, what a marvel it appeared to me, / When I beheld three faces on his head! / The one in front, and that vermilion was;	*Oh, what a marvel it appeared to me, / When I saw three faces on his head! / The one in front was vermillion;*
Two were the others, that were joined with this / Above the middle part of either shoulder, / And they were joined together at the crest;	*The other two joined / Above the middle part of each shoulder, / And were joined together at the crest;*
And the right-hand one seemed 'twixt white and yellow / The left was such to look upon as those / Who come from where the Nile falls valley-ward.	*The right-hand one seemed between white and and yellow; / The left looked like those / Who come from where the Nile falls towards the valley.*
Underneath each came forth two mighty wings, / Such as befitting were so great a bird; / Sails of the sea I never saw so large.	*Underneath each came forth two mighty wings, / Like those of a great bird; / I had never sails of a ship as large.*
No feathers had they, but as of a bat / Their fashion was; and he was waving them, / So that three winds proceeded forth therefrom.	*They had no feathers, but were made like a bat; / And he was waving them, / So that three winds proceeded forth.*
Thereby Cocytus wholly was congealed. / With six eyes did he weep, and down three chins / Trickled the tear-drops and the bloody drivel.	*Thereby congealing all of Cocytus. / With six eyes he wept, and down three chins / Trickled the teardrops and bloody drivel.*
At every mouth he with his teeth was crunching / A sinner, in the manner of a brake, / So that he three of them tormented thus.	*He crunched with the teeth of each mouth / A sinner, in the manner of a brake, / So that he tormented each one alike.*
To him in front the biting was as naught / Unto the clawing, for sometimes the spine / Utterly stripped of all the skin remained.	*In front, the biting was nothing / Compared to the clawing, for sometimes the spine / Was all that was left.*
"That soul up there which has the greatest pain," / The Master said, "is Judas Iscariot; / With head inside, he plies his legs without.	*"That soul up there which has the greatest pain," / The Master said, "is Judas Iscariot; / With his head inside, he plies with his legs.*
Of the two others, who head downward are, / The one who hangs from the black jowl is Brutus; / See how he writhes himself, and speaks no word.	*The other two, who are heads down, / The one who hangs from the black jowl is Brutus; / See how he writhes himself, and can't speak.*
And the other, who so stalwart seems, is Cassius.	*The other one, who seems so stalwart, is Cassius.*

But night is reascending, and 'tis time That we depart, for we have seen the whole."	*But night is near, and it's time That we depart, for we have seen everything."*
As seemed him good, I clasped him round the neck, And he the vantage seized of time and place,	*With gladness, I clasped him around the neck, And having the advantage seized the time and place,*
And when the wings were opened wide apart,	*When the wings were opened wide apart,*
He laid fast hold upon the shaggy sides; From fell to fell descended downward then Between the thick hair and the frozen crust.	*He laid hold on the shaggy sides; Descending downward then Between the thick hair and the frozen crust.*
When we were come to where the thigh revolves Exactly on the thickness of the haunch, The Guide, with labour and with hard-drawn breath,	*When we came to where the thigh revolves On the thickness of the haunch, The Guide, with laboring hard-drawn breath,*
Turned round his head where he had had his legs,	*Turned around his head where he had hold of the legs,*
And grappled to the hair, as one who mounts, So that to Hell I thought we were returning.	*And grappled to the hair, like one who mounts, So I thought we were returning to Hell.*
"Keep fast thy hold, for by such stairs as these," The Master said, panting as one fatigued, "Must we perforce depart from so much evil."	*"Hold on, for stairs like these," The Master said, panting with fatigue, "We must use to depart from such evil."*
Then through the opening of a rock he issued, And down upon the margin seated me; Then tow'rds me he outstretched his wary step.	*Then through the opening of a rock he issued, And down on the margin seated me; Then he outstretched his wary step towards me.*
I lifted up mine eyes and thought to see Lucifer in the same way I had left him; And I beheld him upward hold his legs.	*I lifted up my eyes to see Lucifer in the same way I had left him; And I saw him hold his legs upward.*
And if I then became disquieted, Let stolid people think who do not see What the point is beyond which I had passed.	*And if I didn't become disquieted, Let stolid people think who do not see The point which I had passed.*
"Rise up," the Master said, "upon thy feet; The way is long, and difficult the road, And now the sun to middle-tierce returns."	*"Rise up," the Master said, "on your feet; The way is long and the road is difficult, And now the sun returns to the middle."*
It was not any palace corridor There where we were, but dungeon natural, With floor uneven and unease of light.	*It was not a palace corridor Where we were, but a natural dungeon, With uneven floors and little light.*
"Ere from the abyss I tear myself away, My Master," said I when I had arisen, "To draw me from an error speak a little;	*"Here from the abyss, I tear myself away, My Master," I said, when I had arisen, "To keep me from erring, speak a little;*

Where is the ice? and how is this one fixed Thus upside down? and how in such short time From eve to morn has the sun made his transit?" And he to me: "Thou still imaginest Thou art beyond the centre, where I grasped The hair of the fell worm, who mines the world. That side thou wast, so long as I descended; When round I turned me, thou didst pass the point To which things heavy draw from every side, And now beneath the hemisphere art come Opposite that which overhangs the vast Dry-land, and 'neath whose cope was put to death The Man who without sin was born and lived. Thou hast thy feet upon the little sphere Which makes the other face of the Judecca. Here it is morn when it is evening there; And he who with his hair a stairway made us Still fixed remaineth as he was before. Upon this side he fell down out of heaven; And all the land, that whilom here emerged, For fear of him made of the sea a veil, And came to our hemisphere; and peradventure To flee from him, what on this side appears Left the place vacant here, and back recoiled." A place there is below, from Beelzebub As far receding as the tomb extends, Which not by sight is known, but by the sound Of a small rivulet, that there descendeth Through chasm within the stone, which it has gnawed With course that winds about and slightly falls. The Guide and I into that hidden road Now entered, to return to the bright world; And without care of having any rest We mounted up, he first and I the second, Till I beheld through a round aperture	*Where is the ice and how is this one fixed* *Upside down? How in such a short time* *From evening to morning, has the sun made its way?"* *He replied: "You still imagine* *You are beyond the center, where I grasped* *The hair of the fallen one who mines the world.* *You were on that side, as I descended;* *When I turned around, you didn't pass the point* *To which things draw heavy from every side,* *And now you have come beneath the place* *Which hangs opposite the vast* *Dry land and underneath whose cope was put to death* *The Man, who was born and lived without sin.* *You have your feet on the little sphere* *Which makes the other face of Judecca.* *It is morning here when it is evening there;* *And he who made a stairway with his hair* *Remains fixed as he was before.* *He fell down out of heaven on this side;* *And all the land, that emerged here,* *Made the sea a veil out of fear,* *From our hemisphere; and by chance* *To flee from him, what appears on this side* *Left the place vacant and recoiled back."* *A place below there, recedes as far* *From Beelzebub, as the tomb extends,* *Which is not known by sight, but by the sound* *Of the small river, that descends there* *Through the chasm within the stone, which it has made* *With a course that winds about and slightly falls.* *The Guide and I had now entered that hidden road,* *To return to the bright world;* *And without care of having any rest* *We mounted up, first him then me,* *Until I saw through a round aperture*

Some of the beauteous things that Heaven doth bear;   *Some of the beautiful things from Heaven*

Thence we came forth to rebehold the stars.   *Then we came forth to see again the stars.*

Printed in Great Britain
by Amazon